ANCIENT EGYPT
FROM THE RECORDS

BY

M. E. MONCKTON JONES
M.A., F.R.Hist. Soc.

WITH TWELVE ILLUSTRATIONS
AND TWO MAPS

METHUEN & CO. LTD.
36 ESSEX STREET W.C.
LONDON

First Published in 1924

PRINTED IN GREAT BRITAIN

ANCIENT EGYPT
FROM THE RECORDS

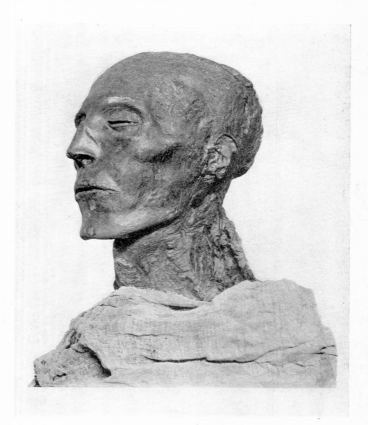

SETI I

PREFACE

THIS story of Ancient Egypt was prepared in the attempt to meet the general desire of a wide public for a simple, readable tale of that " Land of Egypt " with the name of which we all, be we Christian, Moslem, or Jewish readers, have been familiar from childhood, however unlearned. None but an expert Egyptologist can write with authority on this subject ; but every Egyptologist is too much of a scholar and too much absorbed in the quest of the original material to be able to give much attention to the demands of the man in the street. The author has felt that there is not only room but perhaps need for a humbler scribe to select the vital points of the story and to present it so that he who runs—perhaps on other errands—can read.

It is admitted that every new discovery of the explorers modifies our knowledge of Egypt, and the reliable facts can only be had on their security : the words of the records themselves carry, as do those of our own terse Chronicles, the flavour of the bygone life. On both these counts the writer has felt it indispensable to have recourse to the fountainhead of the records, and it is by the kindness of Professor Breasted and the University of Chicago in allowing a very generous amount of citation from the " Records of Ancient Egypt " that this method has been possible. Their permission has enabled the writer to give to an otherwise barren sketch some echo of the words of the very men who played out their part in history so long ago, and it is in the conviction that no readers of those words can fail to be drawn to study Mr. Breasted's treasury of records for themselves that the freedom to use them has been accepted.

But while admitting this paramount debt the writer gladly acknowledges the debts incurred to the many other authorities used—to Professor Petrie, to Dr. Budge, and to the Liverpool School of Egyptology, to whose lecturers, Professors Newberry and Garstang, she owes the first impulse to these studies.

M. E. MONCKTON JONES

BARTON, CAMBS.

November 8, 1923

CONTENTS

LIST OF ILLUSTRATIONS

NOTE.—The models illustrated are from tombs of the XIIth
  Dynasty.

LIST OF ABBREVIATIONS

Br.   = Breasted, "Records of Ancient Egypt."

Petrie = W. Flinders Petrie, "History of Egypt."

Budge = E. A. Wallis Budge, "History of Egypt."

ANCIENT EGYPT FROM THE RECORDS

CHAPTER I

THE OPENING SCENE

IT is clear from the numbers of flint tools and weapons found there, that the great African deserts on which Old Stone Age men lived before the days of historical records were once fertile. Geologists tell us that since that Age changes happened to the form and climate of the country which must have cut off those early men completely from the later Egyptians, glimpses of whose history can be made out from their relics.

The land of Egypt has been called " The Gift of the Nile," for it is the rich mud left by the Nile floods year by year which has made it fit for human life, and no doubt the lush growth of grasses and the plenty of animals that they fed first drew men to its banks to settle and build. Far beyond the long, narrow strip of the valley itself now lie deserts : mile upon mile of bare rock and yellow sands, dry as dust and fruitless as the salt leagues of an ocean.

Like "the unplumbed, estranging sea," these deserts cut men off from touch and sound of those dwelling beyond them. Egypt was like an island, with deserts for sea, and her people grew up alone, so that for many centuries their ways of building and burying, their habits, government, and thoughts bore no marks of foreign making. West of them the great Libyan deserts passed into the vast Sahara ; to the east less arid tracts and granite hills shut them off from the Red Sea and the rains which arise from it. To the south and the hidden sources of their river they must have turned to seek an outlet, but even this was partly blocked by great cataracts, which boats could mount only at certain times of the year. From the first cataract to the Mediterranean their land stretched for 500 miles on each side of the life-giving Nile.

Yet in remote ages four different groups of people had in one way or another found a track across the deserts to this Land of Plenty. History cannot yet tell us about their wanderings ; we can only make guesses about them from the looks of their children's children. One group are of a red-brown colour ; these are called the Egyptians proper. A second group are darker in colour and more like Jews, with fine heads and beaked noses, and must have come in from the East. Quite different from either are the black-skinned, thick-lipped negro people from the south. The fourth group, however, are the fairest of all, fairer even than the Egyptians, with light hair and blue eyes : these came in from the Libyan deserts in the west. In the oldest tombs in Egypt remains of all these four types can be traced, but the most marked likeness is to the Libyans and to the Eastern tribes, such as the Somali and Galla ; and remains six or seven thousand years old are in form not unlike the peasants, or " fellaheen," of to-day.

As in the history of Britain, so in Egypt, the first hint we get of man's life is from his graves. There are in Egypt no grass-covered barrows such as are common in parts of England, but there we can see many different kinds of graves all peculiar to Egypt—from the shallow holes scraped in the sand by the simplest people to the mighty Pyramids known throughout the whole world as the tombs of their early kings.

A hundred years ago it would have puzzled the wisest men to tell how and why the Pyramids were built. To-day we can follow step by step every stage of their making, from the primitive wish to shelter the dead man from wild beast or human insult, through a time when he was thought to need food and tools on his journey to a far country, until stage by stage this developed into a hope that he was living on and needed his possessions for all time.

At first life was no doubt a hard struggle ; men could only seek things needful—food, stone weapons, a rag of clothing—fight for them, enjoy them, and die ; and when the stoutest leader died, his fellows had, we may fancy, scant time to mourn or honour him, and must do what they could in haste and with poor tools. The simplest grave was made—a mere hole scooped out of the ground—covered perhaps with branches, very shallow and easily hidden by the blowing sandstorm of the desert. The body, doubled up with the knees against the chin, with a poor pot or two and perhaps a stone hoe or a string of clay beads laid upon it, was buried in the sand with no covering but that.

In the next stage there is a coffin, but unlike ours. The earliest were round clay vessels like huge pots, just large enough to hold the cramped up body. Soon these were given up for square chests, when wood was used ; and by that time the goods buried with a man, or the little models of them, were set a little apart from his body, not upon or about it as at first.

Before long the burial-place is a squared hole or chamber under ground, the coffin at one end, the goods at the other ; then a partition is placed between them, or two chambers even are reserved for the goods, tools, ornaments, and weapon's, and, since the depth is now greater, a few steps are cut out to lead down to the tomb.

Then comes a new feature : a low, flat mound is built over the tomb, down to which leads a regular flight of steps. With the growth of the building a growth in the idea of the after-life is clearly shown by the nature of the things placed in the tomb. Men were by this time so sure of their tradition of an after-life that they spared no pains to equip their dead relations with all that they had been accustomed to in the earthly life. And now, besides the first supply, the offerings were renewed from time to time, for it was made possible for people to revisit the tombs ; they were no longer sealed up as at first.

The flat-topped mound of brick or stone built over the tomb is called a " Mastaba," and it seems clear that great men often prepared their tombs during their lifetime, like Joseph of Arimathea. Now it would often happen that the mound was completed while the owner still lived and that he wished to add something to the grandeur of the tomb, and so the practice arose of building another story on the top of the mound. This second story was built smaller in plan than the first, and a third, smaller again, was sometimes added, so that by degrees a kind of pyramid of terraces rose above the actual burial-place. The necessaries placed within, too, for the after-life, became more and more carefully modelled on the things he had owned in this, or on what his priest taught him to expect, and so from them the story of the daily life, the habits, and the faith of the Egyptian can be learnt.

As the pyramid plan developed the problem of an entrance to the tomb both easy and secure became more and more difficult. At first it was a mere sloping passage, open to the sky and closed at the sepulchre mouth by a block of stone ; but when the terraces reached beyond the plan of the grave the passage had to be arched over : as the weight above grew greater, so must the supporting arches increase in strength, till at last the sky was quite shut out by a solid roof. In this passage, however, places were left for the great stone portcullises to be lowered to bar the passage and to secure the doorway of the tomb chamber with its treasures. In the greater pyramids two or even three of these massive rock doors were lowered across the entrance-way at intervals, and once lowered were immovable, for by that date it was customary to furnish the grave with all supplies, treasures, and records, and the servants of the Pharaoh were buried round about his tomb ; all would thus accompany the great dead and bear witness for him.

In the pyramid itself all was made ready before the burial, and once the great blocks were lowered into place the tomb was sealed ; some have remained so to our own day, though the secret of others has been forced by successors or robbers. It is to the Pyramids and other graves of Egypt that men have gone to find out what they could of the history of the land. Much has been puzzled out, but much still remains uncertain, confused, or quite unknown.

In the dim mists of 6,000 years ago faint figures seem to move ; scholars read a name here, an action or a portrait there, and can only guess at their connexion. There is no story of other peoples to help, for Egypt seems older than all others, unless perhaps there existed States on the Persian Gulf or in distant Asia whose memory is lost. It is thought that Arabia was peopled by 4000 B.C., and that a group moved round the head of the Persian Gulf and settled on the Euphrates, and probably some of the people in Egypt had come from Arabia too, by way of Sinai ; when this was we do not know.

The first men of whom traces are found in the southern Nile valley were about $5\frac{1}{2}$ feet high, red brown in colour, with narrow " long " head, smooth hair, brown eyes, and slight, slim body. They used stones as tools ; their hoes were sharpened to a smooth edge and set in wooden handles. They could at one time make basketry and pottery, which they burnished till it shone, and coloured crudely ; and in time they learned of copper and tried, not unskilfully, to work it. In the Delta, too, their relics show no mean sense of art and even some hint of astronomical science. Of all the marvels of Egypt none deserves more attention perhaps than the early invention of a calendar.

As early as 4241 B.C. the men of the Delta appear to have learned, partly from watching for the yearly return of the Nile flood, partly from noticing the changing positions of the sunrise, that the days made up a regularly recurring sequence, the year period. They reckoned thirty days to the month, and then added five extra days to the twelfth month and celebrated these as a festival. It is this scheme of theirs which we use to-day in a modified form, and it would have been easier for modern man to correct it to absolute correspondence with the sun's movements had it come to us as it left the Egyptians and not been altered, halfway through the centuries, by the Romans.

Among the mist-wrapped figures of early Egypt looms a god-king, named Horus.   He is as legendary and doubtful a being as our own King Arthur, and with even less of fact within the legend.   " The Scorpion King," or " Re-Harmakhis, king of Ta-sti " in the Eastern Sudan, as this hero was called, with a force of troops from the south, foot-men armed with spears, marched north from " The Land of the Bow " and overcame the stone-users of Middle Egypt, raiding even into the Delta. The hawk was his sacred symbol, but he is also pictured with a winged disk, which some take to represent the sun.   His capital was fixed at Edfu, and he is said to have captured the Vulture-goddess of El Kab, Nekhebet, and her two towns of Nekheb and Nekhen on either bank of the river, twelve miles north of Edfu ; but his rule was stable only in Middle Egypt, if at all.   It fell to his successors to move the capital to Abydos and pass north into the Delta, there beginning to subdue a robuster folk, who may have come from more northern lands.

These were short, square-set men, with broad foreheads, short noses, and black eyes.   Their culture was high, and they had no doubt kinsmen on other shores of the Mediterranean.

The Egyptian dawn is too dim for certainty, but Menes—who may be the same as one named Aha—is a figure no longer legendary, but the first historic Pharaoh and maker of Egypt. He was the first to be given, in about 3400 B.C., the title of " King of the South and North." The kingdom of the South stretched then from Memphis to the first cataract, and his capital was at Abydos ; but he also ruled the northern State of the Delta, with its great cities Sais, Buto, and Busiris, and so was called " The Uniter of the Two Lands." His tomb was made at Nekadah, south of Abydos. In his day the reed symbol of Upper Egypt and the bee of Lower Egypt were used together before the King's name. The lotus and papyrus intertwined upon the throne showed his double rule. In his reign the famous town of Memphis, " the White Wall," was built as a rampart of the South against northern disturbances. The reign is noteworthy, too, as a landmark in the advance of civilization, for Egyptians had already made out of the separate picture-symbols recognized, stereotyped letters, the " first step towards the writing of words," which was soon a complete art.

The proper order of these early kings is not certainly known, but about this time lived a great one, Narmer, possibly the same as Menes, a conqueror, also called " King of the South and North." From among his treasured goods there remains a sculptured sceptre and a " palette " ornament on which his deeds are shown in picture. They tell how the king has " slain thousands " and brought captive prisoners, oxen, and goats by hundreds of thousands ; " he assumed the Red Crown of Lower Egypt " (i.e the Delta). His prisoners were Libyans, who then, as so often later, were constantly menacing and invading the Delta.

All these early Pharaohs of Dynasties I and II had to renew again and again Menes' warfare with the Libyan men, who kept entering the Delta and unsettling it. Memphis was their " White Wall," their stronghold from which they could swing forces levied in the loyal South against the turbulent Northerners. Little by little they gained control and the Delta settled down ; but even in the reign of Khasekhem VI another campaign was needed to subdue revolt there.

Four kings are thought to have followed Menes as Kings of the South and North, and form with him Dynasty I : Semti, also called Den or Ten, Achab, Smerka, and Qa. Their tombs show that there was rapid progress in building and other arts in their days. Semti's tomb was panelled with wood and paved with granite, and two flights of steps from the surface led down to it. A wooden tablet describes events of his reign and shows a figure of the sacred " Henu " boat used in the worship of Seker, the god of Death, at Memphis. On another tablet the king is shown performing the Sed festival of Osiris, dancing before the god, in thanksgiving for a new lease of life. Later Egyptians told that Semti found part of the " Book of

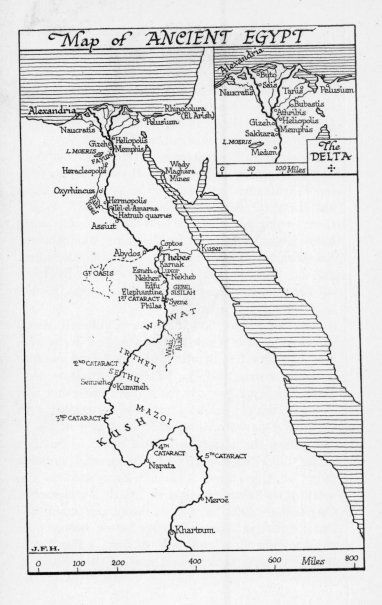

Map of ANCIENT EGYPT

Alexandria
Rhinocolura (El Arish)
Pelusium
Naucratis
Gizeh
Heliopolis
L.MOERIS
Memphis
FAYUM
Heracleopolis
Wady Maghara Mines
Oxyrhincus
Hermopolis
Tel-el-Amarna
Hatnub quarries
Assiut
Coptos
Kuser
Abydos
Thebes
Karnak
Luxor
GT OASIS
Esneh
Nekhen
Nekheb
Edfu
Elephantine
GEBEL SISILAH
1ST CATARACT
Syene
Philae
W A W A T
IRTHET
Wadi Alaki
2ND CATARACT
SETHU
Semneh
Kummeh
K U S H
M A Z O I
3RD CATARACT
4TH CATARACT
5TH CATARACT
Napata
Meroë
Khartoum

J.F.H.

| 0 | 100 | 200 | 400 | 600 | Miles | 800 |

The DELTA

Alexandria
Buto
Sais
Naucratis
Tanis
Pelusium
Bubastis
Athribis
Gizeh
Heliopolis
Sakkara
Memphis
L.MOERIS
Medum

0   50   100 Miles

the Dead " and also a medical recipe, and we may take that to mean at least that he was an enlightened monarch. The picture letters were now fully established, and it becomes tolerably easy for scholars to make out the meaning of words.

King Smerka, or Smerkhal, seems to have carried his arms eastwards into the Sinai country, for he worked the copper mines there which had been made by Semites, and a picture is there on rock of the king braining a native with his mace. Little is known of Qa, the last Pharaoh of this line.

The title of Pharaoh is a Hebrew corruption of Pero, i.e. the Great House of Government. The two kingdoms which formed this early Egypt—the North or Red Land or Delta, and the South or White Land about Abydos—were each of them settled and ordered before they were united. Like the little county kingdoms of our heptarchy, each had its own treasure house and its own scheme of raising money both for the kings and the gods. Egyptian religion was the worship of Nature under various forms, especially the sun ; and the king in each land at first stood as the mouthpiece of his people before the god : he was priest as well as king, and the levies of goods or treasure taken from his people were his by virtue of this double duty of protecting them against their human and superhuman enemies. When the two kingdoms were joined the old names of the Red Land and the White Land were not forgotten, and though the White House became the only treasury, its façade was known as "The Double House," and was sometimes represented by a sign of two houses, while the country always kept its old name "The Two Lands." The treasury was also the storehouse for all the precious and sacred goods used in funeral rites. Specially appointed priests as well as civil officers had charge of the treasury, the provision house, the vineyard, etc.

CHAPTER II

THIRD DYNASTY (2980 B.C.) TO FIFTH DYNASTY

U NDER the Third Dynasty the capital was firmly fixed at Memphis, and among the kings who ruled the Two Lands from there the most notable is Khasekhem, or Khasekhemui, as he later called himself. The first of the remaining Egyptian statues are two of this king—one in slate and one in limestone : they were found in his temple at Herakenpolis. Tombs of the earlier kings varied in size from 20 by 30 feet to 40 by 50 feet ; Khasekhem's measured 223 feet long by 54 feet at its widest. The actual grave was a sunken stone chamber, 10 feet by 17 feet and nearly 6 feet deep, cut into a natural cleft in the rock ; above it were several rows of large and small chambers in which had been placed stone and copper vases, tools of copper as well as of flint, basket work, great pottery jars, stores of grain, and other foods. The statues are fine, simple work, although showing the rules of convention which imply a long art history already passed ; the arrangement of the seated figure is a little stiff and conventional :

13

the feet placed precisely together and the hand palm downwards on the thigh ; the limbs are broadly treated, but the head most carefully finished. The form is slight, the head round and firmly carried with a royal air, wearing the tall mitre-shaped crown of the South. On the vases is an inscription which reads, " The year of fighting the Northern enemy within the city of Nekheb the goddess Nekheb grasps the rebels, and unites Egypt before the Horus Khasekhem."[1]

At the base of each statue is the king's Horus name or sacred title, and round the base are scratched figures of his slaughtered enemies and the number of them, 47,209. These were men of Northern Egypt, with whom we learn from the vase inscriptions and from a scene carved on one of them that Khasekhem VI waged a fierce war before he could reunite the Two Lands of North and South.

Khasekhem VI wedded a lady called En Maat Hap, " She whose orders are always obeyed." On clay seals stamped with names and inscriptions she is called " The king-bearing mother, En Maat Hap," and at a later age she was adored with offerings of 100 loaves, so it has been thought that she was a princess of the North in whom the union was secured and that the next Dynasty owed its origin to her and held her in especial reverence.

Zoser, her son, was a great builder. He put down a rising in Nubia, and seems to have worked

[1] Petrie, p. 27[a²]

the mine' in Sinai, like Semerkhal, for his name
is inscribed there at Wady Maghara. He built
himself two tombs—one of them at Bet Khallâf,
near Abydos, as King of the South. This was a
mastaba of brick, 300 feet by 150 feet. "Within
it is a long passage descending from the top, barred
by five great portcullis blocks of stone, leading to
a wide horizontal passage, and a dozen chambers
at the bottom, which is over fifty feet underground.
A great quantity of broken stone vases, nearly all
of alabaster, were found inside, but not one was
inscribed ; and the only identification of the
builder is from the clay sealings."[1]

The second tomb built by Zoser was a great
novelty in building, for it was made of stone, the
first great stone monument of that tremendous series
of pyramids which have been the most typical
expression of the Egyptian character and remain
unrivalled by any further architecture in the world.
This tomb was built at a point now called Saqqara,
on the west of the river just below Memphis. At
first it was simply a mastaba, flat-topped like the
brick one and only 38 feet high and 227 feet wide ;
but Zoser went on increasing it. First he widened
the ground plan, then added height in proportion
by building upon the original top a smaller one, and
so leaving a terrace round it. This process was
repeated till six steps existed, and the five terraces
have given the pyramid the name of the step or
terrace pyramid of Saqqara ; the final height

[1] Petrie, p. 30[a].

was 195 feet. This reign is also distinguished
by the influence of Imhotep, Egypt's earliest sage,
whose wisdom, shown in magic and medicine and
the utterance of proverbs which the people passed
on from generation to generation, as well as in
planning new architecture, is perhaps the secret
of its greatness.

THE OLD KINGDOM.—DYNASTY IV, 2900 B.C.

With this Dynasty begin the reigns of the great
pyramid builders, of whom the first is Snefru,
though some count him the last of Dynasty III.
Early in his reign he seems to have designed the
making of great buildings, for he raided the Sudan
to capture labour and brought back as captives
7,000 men, as well as great herds of cattle and much
gold. He worked the mines of Sinai for copper
and for turquoise stones, and on the rock is a
portrait of him, like that of Semti, in the act of
slaying a Semite. His shipbuilding too is recorded :
one boat was 100 cubits long, and with sixty others
of smaller size was finished in one year ; another,
of cedar, was built in forty days. They were used
to fetch stone from the Turra limestone quarries.

The result of these activities appeared in two
pyramids, one of which is known as " The Pyramid
of Medum " and the " False Pyramid," because
it is in three stages or terraces. It is fortunate
that the pyramid of Saqqara and this False Pyramid

are still to be seen in their unfinished state, for they show just how the pyramids were built, first in terraces, the successive steps then filled in and the whole finished with a smooth facing of stone. By the time of Snefru it had become the rule with the wealthy classes to have their dead embalmed, and the bodies in their tombs are placed at full length ; but the poorer, humble folk still buried their dead in the old manner and cramped attitude of their forefathers. Adjoining the pyramid of Medum was a small temple, consisting of a courtyard with two chambers, and in this the worship of this king was kept up regularly, even to the period of the Ptolemies. Round about the pyramid were tombs built for the officials of his court and their wives, and some graves of ordinary folk, perhaps servants of his household. From fragments of an inscription a few statements have been made out about a certain " Methen," one of Snefru's officials. He is called " Administrator, Nomarch (provinces were called Nomes), Overseer of Commissions in the Anubis Nome." " There were presented to him . . . things of his father, the judge and scribe, Anubisemonekh ; there was no grain or anything of the house, but there were people and small cattle (i.e. sheep, goats, etc.). He was made chief scribe of the provision magazine and overseer of the things of the provision magazine."[1] In this reign the first fleet of ships sent to Syria for cedar seems to show the expanding power of Egypt.

[1] Br. I, p. 77, ll. 1–5.

2

Snefru had a wife, Merisankh, and a royal favourite, Mertityôtes. The latter survived him ; then she served Khufu, and survived him also. A statue of her is to be seen at Leyden ; it is obviously a good portrait and is valuable, showing that she was of a different and probably lower race than the king.

In art and architecture this reign marks a turning point : in building, wood yields to stone, and there is much wood panelling, while the inscriptions and sculpture in the tombs at Medum are equal to any later work in craftsmanship and beauty.

Khufu (Greek, *Cheops*) is perhaps the best-known name of all the early Pharaohs because of the Great Pyramid that he built, upon which century after century the men of Greece and Rome and Europe and Asia have looked with amazement. But there is little in the story of his reign or those of the whole dynasty to bear out any other claim to greatness. It looks as though all their interest and power had been spent on rearing those enormous monuments, and as if the resources of their lands and the strength of their people had been buried with them in these monstrous tombs. But the Great Pyramid remains. Khufu called it " Khut," or " Glory," a title it deserves by its size. It is higher than any other building that was made in the world up to the last century. It covers $12\frac{1}{2}$ acres of ground, and it probably contained 3,000,000 cubic yards of masonry ; it stood 480 feet high.

According to Herodotus[1] 100,000 men were levied every three months to work upon it, and the stone must have been brought from limestone quarries on the other side of the Nile to Gizeh, where it stands out above eight other monstrous pyramids. It took twenty years to build. The problem of how the great blocks of stone could have been raised to their places has long been a puzzle, but the most probable answer is that the myriads of workmen were set to build steep slopes of mud or sand, and the blocks dragged up these inclines by the use of rollers and short levers and the labour of innumerable gangs of straining men.

Herodotus says that Cheops began by closing the temples and forbidding any sacrifices to be offered, and he then compelled all the Egyptians to work for him. Some of the work is of extraordinarily fine finish.

" The entrance passage and the casing (i.e. outside surface) are perhaps the finest ; the flatness and squareness of the joints being extraordinary, equal to opticians' work of the present day, but on a scale of acres instead of feet or yards of material. The squareness and level of the base is brilliantly true, the average error being less than a ten-thousandth of the side in equality, in squareness, and in level. The queen's chamber is also very finely fitted, the joints being scarcely perceptible. Above that the work is rougher. . . . Apparently the architect who designed and insisted

[1] Herodotus, Bk. I, 177, etc.

on all the fine work died during its progress, and far less able heads were left to finish it."[1]

Another great builder was King Khafre, of whom there are sculptured portraits so lifelike that his face is quite well known. One is a great statue carved in diorite, a very hard crystalline rock. The king is seated on a straight-backed, armless throne, wearing no robes, but his head is sheltered by the wings of the hawk god ; his beard is cut long and straight and his face is dignified and kindly, " combining what a man should be to win our feelings and what a king should be to command our regard."[2] This is one of the best pieces of Egyptian art of any age, and yet one of the earliest. It is a pity that we know no more of the king's life and acts. The pyramid he built beside that of Khufu on the south-west is known as the Second Pyramid. The stone used in it is less good than that used in Khufu's, except some red granite used for the bottom course and the entrance passage. In part the pyramid consists of the natural, un-moved rock of the hillside, much of which has been cut away to leave the pyramid standing clear. To the east of it was a great temple, consisting of two pillared halls, in one of which the statue was found. Part of this temple is still buried and more treasures may be hidden in it. It was decorated with red granite and white alabaster.

Near this pyramid lies the Sphinx. It is a huge outcrop of rock, which had been shaped into an

[1] Petrie, p. 40.   [2] Petrie, p. 54.

immense lion with a man's head, lying couchant
with its paws stretched out before it on the sand.
It is 200 feet long and 70 feet high, and the face was
once painted red.   It was a symbol of the god-
king Re-Harmakhis, with whom the legendary
history of Egypt begins, and who is himself an
image of the sun god, and it is identified with the
ruling Pharaoh—probably Khafre.

Khafre was followed by Menkure, a pious ruler
who was known to the ancient Greeks as Mykerinos.
He built two pyramids, and in later times was
credited with causing much work to be done in
connexion with the " Book of the Dead."

An inscription of about 2700 B.C. tells of the king's
visit to inspect the building of the pyramid and a
tomb beside it.   " As for this tomb, it was the king
of Upper and Lower Egypt, Menkure, who caused
that it be made when his Majesty was upon the road
beside the pyramid, Hir, in order to inspect the work
on the pyramid ' Divine is Menkure ' ; there came
the naval commander and the two high priests of
Memphis, and the workmen, standing upon it, to
inspect the work on the pyramid Divine is Menkure.
. . . 50 men were assigned to do the work on it
every day. . . .   His Majesty commanded that no
man should be taken for any forced labour, except
to do the work on it to his satisfaction."[1]   Menkure
was last but one of this dynasty, which spent all its
energies on pyramid building and did little in the
way of war or law-making or trade.   But we have

[1] Br. I, p. 94, l. 14-p. 95.

to remember that our knowledge is almost all derived from the study of their graves, and it is likely that this may give us a false idea of the important place that religion and tomb culture took in their interests. In their pyramids they did achieve an immortal work, and one unique in its character. Professor Petrie says of the building of this Fourth Dynasty, " The essential feeling of all the earliest work is a rivalry with nature. In other times buildings have been placed either before a background of hills, so as to provide a natural setting to them, or crowning some natural height. But the Egyptian . . . selected a range of desert hills, over a hundred feet high, and then subdued it entirely, making of it a mere pedestal for pyramids, which were more than thrice as high as the native hill on which they stood . . . it seemed a mere platform for the work of man."[1]

Menkure was followed by the three so-called Sons of Re : " Se Re " whose advent had been prophesied in the days of Khafre. Legend said their mother was the wife of User-Re, a priest of Re the Heliopolitan sun god, the local god of Heliopolis. In this legend is the expression of a royal or priestly claim that all kings should derive directly from him, as their bodily father, which would greatly increase the power of his priesthood. It is clear from the broad outline of events that with this rising power of the priesthood the royal power gradually lessened. Menkure, Userkaf, and their

[1] Petrie, p. 66, l. 7.

successors were by no means the equals of Khufu, if their works are any test. Indeed, from the time of Khafre the steady expansion of the trade and sway of Egypt is checked, and we hear of no new ventures like those of the Old Kingdom. This in itself is a negative sign of decline. The power of the cult of Re, however, once it begins to play a part in State affairs, goes on constantly growing and becomes the deciding factor in Egyptian history. Kings are great or weak in proportion as they are aided or thwarted by the priests of Re-amen.

Before Menkure's accession the name of Re had already appeared as part of the king's name, and this may mean that already the priests had begun to encroach on the political power. The legend of User-Re was no doubt of their devising; it declares that King Khufu once ordered a magician of his court to fetch certain writings from Heliopolis. This the mage refused to do, for he said that the eldest of three sons to whom Rut tetet should give birth would bring them. When the king asked " Who is this Rut tetet ? " he was answered : " She is the wife of User-Re, priest of Re of Sakhabu, but her three children are in truth the sons of Re himself, and the eldest shall be high priest of Re, his father." When the king heard this he was plunged in sadness. At the birth of the boys the goddess Isis, the Ram-god, Khemu, and three other goddesses appeared, and the children received from them the names, User-kaf, Sahure, and Kakaa, and it was foretold that each of them

in turn should rule over the Two Lands of
Egypt.[1] In this legend there would seem to be preserved the memory of a change both in the religion
and in the line of kings of Egypt ; the change was a
gradual one, which only became complete with the
rule of the Fifth Dynasty. The god Re was one
of the " Pillar " gods, or " idols of stone " adored
by the peoples of Syria and other eastern lands.

The three " Sons of Re " duly ascended the
throne. The first, Userkaf, is little but a name in
the records ; the second, Sahure, is shown on a
bas-relief at Wady Magharah, clubbing a native
in Sinai, like Semti and Snefru. We have another
glimpse of him in an inscription of an official's tomb,
" His Majesty caused that there be brought for him
two false doors from Troja (modern Tura) of stone,
that they be laid in the audience hall of the house,
' Sahure shines with crowns,' and that the two
high-priests of Memphis, and the artizans of the
[———] be assigned to them, that the work on them
might be done in the presence of the king himself.
The stonework went on every day ; there was an
inspection of that which was done on them in the
court daily. His Majesty had colour put on them,
and had them painted in blue."[2]

The monuments of these kings differed a good
deal from the great pyramids of the Fourth Dynasty.
The sun god kings built much smaller pyramids, but
placed beside them gorgeous temples to Re built

[1] After Budge, "History of the Egyptian People," p. 43.
[2] Br. I, p. 109.

on the following plan : At the west end of a large
square court stood a blunted pyramid, on the top
of which was a stone pillar or obelisk. Beside this,
facing the east, was an altar where victims were
sacrificed, and their blood ran down into vessels
placed on the north side. This worship of Re was
the national religion of Egypt under the Fifth
Dynasty, and his priests claimed that Re was the
Supreme Lord of the Afterworld. But their sway
did not last unchallenged beyond the Sixth
Dynasty, when the worship of Osiris began to
rival it.

The Egyptian gods were legion, and their
characters and powers are impossible to distinguish.
The first set of them seem to be the " totems " of
the early tribes—gods who are represented by the
forms of some creature which the tribe has adopted
through fear or pride as their emblem : Sekhmet,
the lioness ; Nekhbet, the vulture ; Khumu, the
ram ; Anubis, the jackal ; Sebek, the crocodile.

Later, if we may accept the stories given by
Plutarch, the Egyptians made various attempts at
grasping the meaning of their world : the long
narrow valley, the overarching sky, studded with
stars at night or blazing blue as their Nile water in
the daytime led them to frame traditions. The sky
was a sea suspended over them and the life-giving
sun sailed over it daily, returning at night by an
underground river to the east. Or they imagined
forms in the night sky—a woman leaning over the
earth, arrayed in stars, whose child was the sun ;

or a vast cow whose calf the sun was. Their land
was a man god, Keb, lying full length ; their river
coming ceaselessly out of the south to flow into the
northern sea must enter a great circle of waters—
Ocean—and so return to its place, and this circular
stream therefore was the ring that bound the earth
on all sides. This circular ocean was the beginning
of all things ; there appeared upon it an egg or
a flower bud from which rose the sun god Re ; from
him four elemental children, earth and sky, air and
water—Keb, Nut, Shu, and Tefnut. The two
latter thrust the former apart, but from these were
born Osiris, Isis, Set, and Nephthys.

Osiris succeeded Re as king, but was slain by Set.
His sister-wife, Isis, recovered his body, and with
the help of Anubis, the jackal who embalmed it,
brought it back to an eternal life in the underworld
as King of the Dead. The son of Isis, Horus,
avenged his father on Set and became in his turn
the sun king.

To reconcile these traditions and to find place
among them for the various nature gods or tribal
totems worshipped zealously each in his own
district was the work of the various priesthoods,
among which that of Re and Amen, or Amon,
finally became supreme. A mythology so full of
confusion and contradiction could give little moral
aid, one would think. Yet the Egyptians were, on
the whole, a righteous and peaceable, industrious
folk. They were essentially practical and artistic,
loving the beauty of nature, and learning no doubt

from this the peaceable, law-abiding habits which are common among a simple peasant folk throughout the world. Contact with nature too led them to ponder on the creative power, and as their culture increased their sages developed a more and more spiritual interpretation of the main themes of their creeds. The sun-disk stood not merely for the sun itself, but for the life and heat-giving power of which the sun was the plainest seal. The love of Isis stood for the self-forgetting devotion of woman, and out of it came the power to cleanse and renew, so that, in the new-born Osiris, Egyptians could worship one who had, and could bestow upon his followers, a new and eternal life. It speaks highly for the moral sense of Egypt that to this exponent of the power of love and suffering to redeem was given the right to judge the souls of the departing and allot them their place in the after-life. References to these creeds were recorded in the famous Book of the Dead, a collection of formulæ with which the dead was provided, either written and pictured in his coffin, on the walls of his tomb, or on rolls buried with him, to guide his entrance into the after-life.

The attitude of the bereaved and the care taken in disposing of the noble at his death is illustrated, in an account of the death of the architect Weshptah, about 2700 B.C.

From the reign of Neferirkere, who succeeded Sahure, this pathetic incident has come down to us in a vivid, disjointed inscription on the tomb of the royal architect. It brings out the close and kindly relation between the Pharaohs and their courtiers under the old order.

The death of Weshptah :

"Neferirkere came to see the beauty of Weshptah's last building . . . and they wondered very greatly . . . Then, lo, his majesty praised him because of it.

"His majesty saw him however that he heard not. . . . When the royal children and companions, who were of the court, heard, great fear was in their hearts.

"He was conveyed to the court and his majesty had the royal children, companions, ritual priests and chief physicians come. . . . His majesty had brought for him a case of writings (medical). They said before his majesty that he was lost. The heart of his majesty was exceedingly sad beyond everything. . . ."[1]

The seventh king of this line was Dedkere-Isesi (Zet), who probably worked the copper mines at Wady Hammamat as well as at Wady Magharah, and used the trade route from the Nile to the Red Sea, for his name is carved on the rocks at the mines. He also sent an officer to the land of Punt (probably Somaliland) to fetch a pygmy, for which the king gave him a rich reward. On their tombs his officials recorded their careers, but these do not tell much for, like British monuments of the eighteenth century, the lines are mainly filled with

[1] Br. I, p. 112, ll. 6, 9, 10-19.

TOMB OF ANTEF, A COURTIER, SHOWING WOODEN MODELS IN COFFIN

the perfections of the dead man ; still they hint
at the stage of order and prosperity which Egypt
reached under these kings. The country is clearly
divided into provinces and at peace, though justice
and comfort seem to be remarkable rather than
normal conditions. Of a private citizen, Nezemib,
it is written : " I was a master of secret things. . . .
Never was I beaten in the presence of any official
since my birth, never did I take the property of any
man by violence ; I was a doer of that which
pleased all men."[1]

Of the Nomarch Henku we are told more : " O
all ye people of the Cerastes Mountain (the twelfth
nome of Upper Egypt) O ye great lords of other
nomes, who shall pass by this tomb, I, Henku, tell
good things : . . . I gave bread to all the hungry
of the Cerastes Mountain ; I clothed him who was
naked there ; I filled its shores with large cattle
and its lowlands with small cattle. . . . I was lord
and overseer of southern grain in this nome. . . . I
settled the feeble towns in this nome with people
of other nomes ; those who had been peasant serfs
therein, I made their offices as officials. I never
oppressed one in possession of his property, so that
he complained of me because of it to the god of my
city ; I spake and told that which was good ;
never was there one fearing because of one
stronger than he, so that he complained because
of it to the god. I speak no lie, for I was one
beloved of his father, praised of his mother, excel-

[1] Br. I, p. 125, 126, ll. 22–16.

lent in character to his brother, and amiable to his sister. . . ."[1]

The last phrases of this epitaph are found on many others in later reigns and may be merely conventional expressions.

The last king of the Fifth Dynasty, Unis, was a great quarrier of stone at Wady Hammamat, and built a pyramid differing from all others in its beautiful decorations.   The walls inside are covered with texts from the religious creeds of all the preceding periods of Egyptian history.   The hieroglyphs in which they are cut are inlaid with a green plaster and the series is of the greatest use in showing what the Egyptian religions had been.   From this reign too " The Proverbs of Ptahhotep " are said to date.

[1] Br. I, p. 126, l. 14–p. 127.

CHAPTER III

SIXTH DYNASTY (2500 B.C.)

OF the Sixth Dynasty the first really important ruler was the king Merire, Pepi I. Under him the country grew well ordered and wealthy, and he carried his arms boldly into the surrounding lands and punished the Sand-dwellers or Bedwin, the Aamu. The epitaph of his officer Uni gives vivid pictures of the campaign, describing the gathering of troops from all Egypt, from Libya, and negroes from the Sudan. We see the way-farer plodding in the hot sand on his sandals, carrying his dough ready mixed for making into bread ; the village with its goats grazing beyond the clustered huts ; the fortified city with its fig trees growing against the houses and its vines clambering over the walls ; and we see the trium-phant return with long lines of weary captives tramping northwards into servitude, perhaps to labour at pyramid building or do the menial tasks of fanning, water-drawing, and so on.

The inscription[1] tells how Uni had come to man's estate, or "fastened on the girdle," under the

[1] Br. I, pp. 141-4.

previous king and helped in the temple building in the quarry of Troya until " his majesty caused that I came downstream " ; then " under the majesty of Pepi " he was appointed to the rank of companion and " inferior prophet of his pyramid city. . . . He loved me more than any servant of his. I heard, being alone with the chief judge and vizier, in every private matter, in the name of the king, of the royal harem and of the six courts of justice, because the king loved me more than any noble of his, more than any servant of his. . . . I did so that his majesty praised me, when preparing the king's journey, when making stations, I did throughout so that his majesty praised me for it above everything. . . . When legal procedure was instituted in private in the harem against the queen, Imtes, his majesty caused me to enter in order to hear alone. . . .

" His majesty made war on the Asiatic Sand-dwellers and his majesty made an army of many ten thousands : in the entire South southward to Elephantine, and northward to Aphroditopolis ; in the Northland on both sides entire in the stronghold, and in the midst of the strongholds, among the Irthet negroes, among the Mazoi negroes, the Yam negroes, among the Warwat negroes, among the Kau negroes, and in the land of Temeh. . . . I was the one who made for them the plan. . . . Not one thereof plundered dough or sandals from the wayfarer ; not one thereof took bread from any city ; not one thereof took any goat from any people. . . . I despatched them. . . . I inspected the number of these troops although never had any servant inspected.

" This army returned in safety, it had hacked up the land of the Sand-dwellers. . . . it had destroyed the land of the Sand-dwellers . . . it had over-turned its strongholds . . . it had cut down its figs and its vines ; it had thrown fire on all its troops . . . it had slain troops therein in many ten thousands . . . it had carried away therefrom a great multitude as living captives. His majesty praised me on account of it above everything.

" His majesty sent me to despatch this army five times, in order to traverse the land of the Sand-dwellers at each of their rebellions, with these troops.

" When it was said there were revolters because of a matter among these barbarians in the land of Gazelle nose I crossed over in troopships with those troops, and I voyaged to the back of the height of the ridge (Highlands of Southern Palestine) on the north of the Sand-dwellers. When this army had been brought in the highway, I came and smote them all and every revolter among them was slain."

This heavy punishment of the last revolt closes the story of Pepi's reign, but the great official continued to serve his heir, Mernere. The warlike work of Pepi, however, seems to have been quite thorough, and the land had peace because of it ; for Uni is now busy with useful governing ; collecting taxes, keeping peace, and doing justice and forwarding the work on the tombs. With only one warship he is able to convey a fleet of cargo-boats up the Nile to Elephantine, in the half-settled Sudan to fetch slabs of granite. To build boats his men hew down the graceful, sweet-scented acacia trees ; they pass upstream from among the dignified, civilized men of Egypt to the restless, half-savage negroes of Ibhet, of Wawat and Yam, who toil in crowds to haul the timber from the forests to the river side. And then comes his crowning achievement : before the new fleet which he had built with the help of the Sudanese tribes, " launched and laden with granite blocks," could be brought downstream he had to cut five great canals at the first cataract. Such work is the best possible proof of the might and authority of the Sixth Dynasty kings, and though neglected for a time became of use a thousand years later to Sesostris III and Thutmose III. These works are described in Uni's tomb inscription[1] as follows :

" When I was master of the footstool of the palace and sandal bearer (the king) . . . made me count and governor of the South. . . . I acted as governor of the South to his satisfaction. Not one therein strove with his neighbour. I accomplished all tasks ; I numbered everything that is counted to the Court in this South twice ; all the (road-making) tax that is counted to

[1] Br. I, pp. 147-150.

the Court in this South twice . . . never before
was the like done in this South.

" His majesty sent me to Ibhet (? Aswan)
to bring the sarcophagus ' Chest of the Living '
and the costly, splendid capstone for the pyramid
called ' Merenre shines and is beautiful.'

" His majesty sent me to Elephantine. . . .
Then I sailed downstream to the pyramid . . . with
six cargo-boats, three tow-boats and three [——]
boats to only one warship. Never had Ibhet and
Elephantine been visited in the time of any kings
with only one warship. . . . His majesty sent me
to Hatnub (alabaster quarry) to bring a huge
offering table of hard stone (not alabaster) of
Hatnub. I brought down this offering table for
him in only seventeen days, it having been quarried
in Hatnub, and I had it proceed downstream in this
cargo-boat (the description of which follows).
I hewed for him a cargo-boat of acacia wood of
60 cubits in its length, and 30 cubits in its breadth,
built in only 17 days, in the third month of the
third season. Although there was no water on
the [? sandbanks] I landed in safety at the pyramid
" Merenre shines and is beautiful." . . .

" His majesty sent me to dig five canals in the
South and to make three cargo-boats and four
tow-boats of acacia wood of Wawat. Then the
negro chiefs of Irthet, Wawat, Yam, and Mazoi
drew timber therefor, and I did the whole in only
one year. They were launched and laden with
very large granite blocks for the pyramid. . . .

I then [——] for the palace in all these five canals.
. . . I was one beloved of his father, and praised
of his mother; firstborn . . . pleasant to his
brothers, the count, the real governor of the South,
revered of Osiris, Uni."

It is clear that both the religious and the civil
services were by this time highly organized and
the officers in each graded in many ranks. We have
a detailed account of another of Mernere's nobles,
Harkhuf, who held the important post of " caravan
leader " in succession to his father, Iri " the sole
companion, the ritual priest." This rank of " sole
companion " is a not uncommon title, and not more
curious than our own " Knight Companion of the
Bath." Harkhuf was perhaps of similar station to
a great Arab sheik of to-day; his work was to take
charge of expeditions to explore and open up trade
with the remote parts of the southern Sudan. His
records are even richer than Uni's in graphic
pictures of the life of his day; such are the reference
to the 300 asses laden with incense, ebony, grain,
panthers, and ivory which he brings back from his
travel; to the master of the bath, Khuni, borne up
against the stream to bring him a royal welcome
as he re-enters Egypt; much as if the king to-day
were to send an admiral in his flagship to escort
a returning explorer from the Antarctic or the
wilds of Brazil.

Harkhuf was sent again and again, and found
himself obliged to take a hand in the local warfare
of the tribes and settle terms of peace between

them. He penetrated finally to a region, perhaps
in Upper Nubia, which he describes as " the western-
most corner of heaven " and " the land of spirits "
and brings back with him a dwarf to dance before
the god (or the new king, Pepi II, who may have
been still a child at this date). So great was Pepi's
delight on hearing of this novelty that he wrote a
letter to the caravan leader to thank him, bidding
him take the utmost care of his prize, and assuring
him that all the officials of the towns on his home-
ward route had orders to purvey all that the
travellers might need " without stint." In our
own day explorers still find tribes of pygmies in the
heart of Africa ; and perhaps to Pepi's childish
eagerness was added the urgency of some learned
courtiers anxious like modern professors to secure
from this survival of an elder age some knowledge of the past of other races. His eagerness
still for all time rings in the words cut on his
servant's tomb : " My majesty desires to see this
dwarf more than all the gifts of Sinai and Punt."

Two more records relate the activity of the
times : an Elephantine noble, bearing the half-
royal name of " Pepinakht," tells of the recovery of
the body of another caravan conductor, En-enkhet,
" who was building a ship " on the coast of the
Red Sea, " for Punt when the Asiatics belonging
to the Sand-dwellers slew him, together with a
troop of the army, which was with him."[1] It is
like one of the telegrams that we read every now

[1] Br. I, p. 163.

and then in the morning paper telling of some
sudden disaster on the frontiers of our Empire—
a tiny party of surveyors ambushed and destroyed
by border tribes or a small outpost sniped and
rushed before help could reach them ; for Egypt
stood to the wild tribes beyond her deserts much
as Great Britain stands to the backward races
overseas as the civilizing, trading paramount power
of her day.

Another official, Sebni, tells of the death of his
father, Mekhu, the " sole companion " of Pepi II
among the Sudanese, and of his own expedition to
rescue the body and bring back with it the fruit
of his father's travels.

(Part of the letter of King Pepi II to Herkhuf,
recorded on his tomb :)[1] . . " Come northward
to the Court immediately ; . . . thou shalt bring
this dwarf with thee, which thou bringest living,
prosperous, and healthy from the land of spirits,
for the dances of the god, to rejoice and gladden
the heart of the king of Upper and Lower Egypt,
Neferkere (Pepi II) who lives for ever. When
he goes down with thee into the vessel, take care
lest he fall into the water. When he sleeps at night
appoint excellent people, who shall sleep beside
him in his tent ; inspect ten times a night. My
majesty desires to see this dwarf more than the
gifts of Sinai and of Punt. If thou arrivest at
Court this dwarf being with thee alive, prosperous
and healthy, my majesty will do for thee a greater

[1] Br. I, p. 161, ll. 4-18.

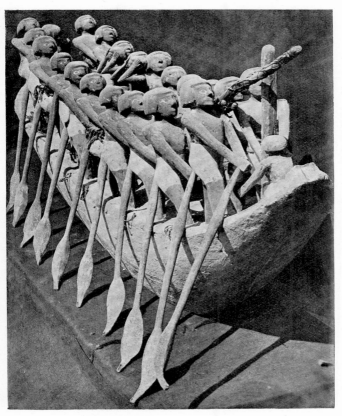

MODEL OF ROWING BOAT OF TWENTY OARS

thing than was done for the treasurer of the god, Burded (Balverdedu) in the time of Sesi, according to the heart's desire of my majesty to see this dwarf.

" Commands have been sent to the chief of the New Towns, the companion and superior prophet, to command that sustenance be taken from him in every store city and every temple, without stinting therein."

(Sebni's expedition to recover his father's body from negroes :)[1] " Then came the ship captain, Intef . . . to give information that . . . Mekhu was dead. . . . Then I took a troop of my estate, and 100 asses with me, bearing ointment, honey, clothing, oil, and [——] of every sack, in order to make presents [in] these countries. . . . I pacified these countries. . . . I loaded the body of this sole companion upon an ass, and I had him carried by the troop of my estate. I made for him a coffin . . . I sent the royal attendant Iri, with two people of my estate . . . bearing incense, clothing . . . one tusk in order to give information . . . and that I had brought this my father and all kinds of gifts from these countries. . . . When I descended . . . behold, Iri came from the court. . . . He brought . . . embalmers, the chief ritual priest . . . the mourners, and all offerings of the White House. He brought festival oil from the Double White House and secret things . . . and all the burial equipment which is issued from the

[1] Br. I, pp. 166-8.

Court. . . . I buried this my father in his tomb
of the necropolis ; "

All these nobles of Elephantine held the onerous
post of Keepers of the Door against the turbulent
negro tribes of Nubia. They were not, like the
lords of the Fourth Dynasty, grouped about the
palace at Memphis, but had their homes at Elephantine, and their graves are cut in the cliffs
which overlook it and the modern Assuan. Suan
means "market," and this point had from time
" to which the memory of man runneth not " been
the scene of barter between the river-man of
Egypt and the negroes, who brought ivory, ebony,
gold, myrrh, and the skins of panthers from their
forests.

Now in the Sixth Dynasty the Pharaohs hold
firmly this key to the southern trade, Mernere
himself making a journey thither as a demonstration : " The coming of the king himself, appearing
behind the hill-country (of the cataract) that
he might see that which is in the hill-country, while
the chiefs of Mazoi, Irthet, and Wawat did obeisance and gave great praise."[1]

King Pepi II, as has been said, was a child aged
only six when he ascended the throne, but he lived
to be a hundred, and so his reign of ninety-four
years is the longest known to history. Such a
long reign is not an unmixed blessing for the country,
since the infirmity of old age makes the monarch
unable to control whatever forces endanger the

[1] Br. I, p. 146, l. 2.

central authority. Under the old King Pepi II the great nobles were able to strengthen their hold of their nomes more and more until they had sapped the life of the kingship and left it little but an empty show. Thus Mernere II, who followed Pepi II, seems to have reigned only a year and entire disorder then ensued as far as can be understood.

In the long history of Egypt no chapter is more difficult to decipher or more fully worth deciphering than this of the Old Kingdom. It was the first firm State on the Nile strong enough to have trade dealings with other lands ; its kings, both in form and power, show the vigour of youth, though in art and in government as well as in architecture their doings reach a magnificent prime never surpassed. It is worth while then to try to see more clearly the picture of Egyptian life under the Old Kingdom in all its ranks and interests.

The scene of the kings' State is at Memphis not far above Cairo, where the stream flows slowly through the mud-plain it has made. Below the city, on the east bank, are the limestone hills from which the stone for the early pyramids was cut and carried to places across the river all along the fifty miles between the Delta and the Fayum oasis. There the pyramids rose, from the first trials at Saqqara and Medum to the Great Pyramid of Gizeh almost at the Delta base. Up and down that fifty miles Pharaoh's men and Pharaoh's boats plied incessantly. On either bank the rich fields were watered by carefully arranged systems of channels to drain the marshes and feed the drier ground. Such works must have been done in the earliest reigns for the country to have yielded the wealth which is evident under these kings. There in the fields and marshes the peasant serfs laboured for Pharaoh, under the direction of the lords to whom he allotted the care of the various districts, or nomes. These may once have been little separate States which Menes and his successors wrought into one, much as our Egbert and Alfred brought the little Saxon kingdoms together. The lords were Pharaoh's officers and held their places for life, and it was not till the Fifth Dynasty that they began to pass on their districts to their children, inheritance going normally to the eldest daughter. They were till then closely bound to the court, having their town houses at Memphis, and being buried in mastaba tombs clustered about the sovereign's pyramid. They lived in fine homes, surrounded by beautiful courts and gardens, and adorned with sculpture and painting. They fished in the river and marshes, hunted deer or oxen on the desert, or sported with their family in hall or garden. Their work was well done too ; they gathered in the food or wealth for Pharaoh and seem to have acted fairly by the people, having to judge as well as tax them and keep the peace among them. Of this work their scribes, trained to write in the cursive hand, in which the picture-hieroglyphs had been reduced to quickly formed letters, kept careful records on tablets or rolls of flattened papyrus, sitting cross-legged at dictation, as may be seen from the scribes' statue in the Louvre. Another figure the sculptors have given us is the overseer, " the Sheikh al Beled," as it was called by the worker who found it ; a typical, stout, sturdy man of business, hard and prosperous, one who will clearly " stand no nonsense " from his workmen. These serfs seem to have had laborious but not unhappy lives. They are pictured at work harvesting the papyrus-reeds in the marshes ; ploughing with a yoke of two oxen ; singing to the sheep as they lead them to tread in the seed, wading across a channel with oxen, one of them carrying a calf on his shoulders. These were the farm-labourers, the greatest mass ; but there were the families of potters, not yet using a wheel ; the men who made marvellously perfect vessels of stone by drilling out the inside ; shipbuilders whose blows seem to resound as we look at them sitting astride the timbers and swinging their club-shaped mallets or whirling their drills, while others heave great axes to split the rough tree-trunk. The boats are similar in shape from the very earliest pre-dynastic painting all through this period— wide and shallow, like punts, but with the tilt fore and aft of a canoe. They made improvements in size mainly, King Snefru having barges built of 100 cubits to carry the weighty stones for his pyramid. Egypt was short of wood, and so light skiffs were made of reeds tied in bundles, while the royal ships came to be built of woods from abroad—from Punt (Somaliland ?) or Palestine.

Metal was known and worked from early days, copper being mined in Sinai ; and gold also was found, though silver was the most precious, as it could only be brought from the Isles of the Sea, the shores of the Mediterranean. Exquisite work was wrought by the gold- and coppersmiths, and no modern ornaments can excel some of their crowns and necklaces, while the carpentry, inlay, and glaze were as exquisitely exact and finished as the marvellous work of the great builders was accurate.

In the matter of decorous clothing, the Egyptians had reached the minimum. Nobles wore a short skirt or kilt from the waist to the knee, a necklace, collar, or chain of office, and a wig, and carried a long staff. Their ladies wore a single, almost transparently fine, garment of linen or silk, fitting closely from the breast to the ankles, but leaving the neck and arms bare. Peasants' wives wore an armless garment straight from neck to ankle, of which the bodice was merely a narrow strip front and back—unless they were engaged on hot, arduous work, when they went bare ; while the men rarely troubled with more than a breech-cloth. In the perfect, warm, dry climate they were thus able to enjoy the utmost comfort, and could paddle in the water channels or lakes with little trouble.

They fed very well. Fish of all kinds, venison,

game, especially wild fowl, as well as meat were plentiful : " sixteen kinds of bread and cake, six kinds of wine, four kinds of beer " are mentioned ; and the well-watered gardens produced all sorts of vegetables, gourds, and fruit ; vine, fig tree, cucumber, melon, and the commoner things ; lentil, peas, beans, and grain of all sorts, while from the palms came harvests of dates, one of the commonest foods.

CHAPTER IV

PERIOD OF DISORDER : DYNASTIES VII TO XI

NO clear story of the so-called Dynasties from VII to XII remains. But even the kings of Dynasty VI have no tombs of the great nobles round about their own, and it looks as though these powerful governors and viceroys of provinces had taken to having courts of their own and passing on their power to their sons until they rivalled the Pharaohs, as Norman sheriffs and Counts Palatine threatened to do in Stephen's reign. Possibly they grouped themselves around rival Pharaohs, for the cities of Memphis and of Herakleopolis (called in the Old Testament Khanes) seem to have been the seats of kings with equal power. No monuments of the time remain to tell us, and this in itself suggests that warfare led to the destruction of any that were made, and the country seems for a long time to have suffered from the complete breakdown of the rule of the Pharaohs. Memphis still laid claim to the first authority, but could not enforce it ; for at Siut and Thebes, as well as at Herakleopolis, men ruled the districts lying north

or south of their cities. Out of the turmoil it was
the men of Khanes who first stand clear. They
fought fiercely with the men of Thebes, and were
aided in their struggle by a notable family of
Nomarchs of Lycopolis. A few fragments from
their records suggest the course of the struggle
and the gradual re-establishment of order by the
kings of Khanes in their own districts. These are
from the period of Dynasties IX and X.

Record of Tefibi, ruler of the Lycopolite Nome
at Siut :[1] " I was one of excellent plans, one useful
to his city, one friendly of face towards a petition
. . . of open face to the widow. . . . I was a
Nile . . . when night came, he who slept on the
road gave me praise, for he was like a man in his
house ; the fear of my soldier was his protection."

This Tefibi passed on his rule to his son " as a
child of a cubit high." He tells of fighting to
enforce the Herakleopolitan rule : " I ceased not
to fight to the end, making use of the south wind
as well as the north wind, of the east wind as well
as of the west wind. He [i.e. the enemy] fell in
the water, his ships ran aground, his army were
like bulls . . . with tails to the front (of the
pursuer)."

Kheti, son of the above Tefibi : " Thou hast
put fear in the land, thou hast chastised Middle
Egypt . . . all the people were in terror, the
villages in panic, fear entered into their limbs."

" How beautiful is that which happens in thy

[1] Br. I, pp. 181–9.

time. . . . Every official was at his post, there
was no one fighting, nor any shooting an arrow.
The child was not smitten beside his mother, the
citizen beside his wife. There was no evil doer . . .
nor any one doing violence."

Kheti II (son of the above) : " I was rich in
grain. When the land was in need, I maintained
the city with ' Kha ' and with ' haket ' (measures
of grain). I allowed the citizen to carry away
for himself grain ; and his wife, the widow and her
son. I remitted all imposts which I found counted
by my fathers. I filled the pastures with cattle,
every man had many colours, the cows brought
forth twofold, the folds were full of calves. I was
kind to the cow when she said ' It is [———], I was
one rich in bulls." . . .

In spite of the temporary importance of these
Herakleopolitan kings under whom Tefibi fought,
a greater power was to grow up south of them at
Thebes, while in the north, at Memphis, the descendants of the ancient Pharaohs still maintained
their hold of a small region. There were thus at
least four different groups of rulers at this period—
at Herakleopolis and Siut, at Memphis and at
Thebes—of whom the Thebans become the most
powerful at last.

Thebes had been merely a country town under
the Old Kingdom, but the region to which it gave
name was at a turning-point of the Nile, at its
nearest to the Red Sea and from Coptos ; a few
miles downstream a break in the eastern hills made

the gateway to the Hammamat sea route ; another sixty miles downstream led to the Sacred Valley of Abydos ; but above all the district was rich by reason of the widening of the valley. It was natural then that in this pleasant valley, so well placed for trade, a powerful family should assume independence during the disorders of the 300 years that followed the collapse of the Old Kingdom.

The Nomarch Intef was the first to emerge as an independent prince. Nomarchs of this famous region had been employed as Counts Palatine to hold this frontier district against raids of the Nubians, the " Nine Bows " or the eastern tribes ; they received the title of " Keeper of the Door " of the South and even more than other great feudal nobles of the time they were empowered to raise the taxes, levy troops, and execute justice. It was an easy step then to independence, and a stele remains showing Intef followed by his hounds like any small country noble, but relating great conquests of the valley below him : " I drove in the mooring-stake (i.e. landed) in the sacred valley. I captured the entire Thinite nome. I opened all her fortresses. I made her the Door of the North."[1] He thus ruled from Thebes to Abydos at least, and a further record describes him as ruler " up river as far as Thes and down river as far as Thinis," just below Abydos. A second Intef succeeded him, and then Mentuhotep I, who seems to have been of his kin, and may be called the Conqueror of Egypt.

[1] Br. I, p. 200, ll. 12-16.

He is shown on a temple fragment from Gebelen smiting four enemies—an Egyptian, a Nubian, an Asiatic, and a Libyan, and this king, for such the Theban Nomarchs have now become, is described as " binding the chiefs of the Two Lands, capturing the South and the Northland, the highlands and the two regions, the Nine Bows and the Two Lands."[1] Such a description can apply with truth only to one who has put himself in the place of Pharaoh, as indeed this Theban house had now done. Controlling the South from Elephantine they had been able to raise such a force as to master the resistance offered at Herakleopolis and once more to unite all the Two Lands of Egypt under one sceptre. The Egyptians slain in this conflict were the last victims of the long civil wars, and a period of more complete and general welfare set in for the people of all classes than they had ever enjoyed.

The further history of the first group of Theban kings is not clear in detail, but their progress can be broadly traced, and the succession, if not regular, was apparently peaceable. Their origin as local princes seems to have taught them to understand their subjects' needs better than the early Pharaohs. Under the Theban dynasties it is the material welfare of land and people which is made the main object of the rulers.   Irrigation works, the measurement of the Nile levels, the reclaiming of land, the working of the mines, trade with Nubia and Punt and later with northern and eastern neighbours,

[1] Br. I, p. 204, ll. 14–16.

assessment of lands and population—such are the interests of these kings, and they result in great bettering of the people's lives and in the growth of a great middle class of prosperous landholders, tradesmen, and craftsmen. The produce of Egypt is not any longer squandered on the things which give no material return, but on raising the standard of comfort. This was no doubt a natural reaction after the lean years of anarchy, just as the Tudor prosperity of England was reaction from the feudal wars ; but the closer tie between prince and people must not be overlooked.

The early Thebans did not build great pyramids, though that of Mentuhotep III at Der-el-Bahri on the west bank near Thebes was of very fine workmanship, and we learn much from its inscriptions. It was built by a sculptor, called Mertisen, who thus recounts his prowess : (I) " know the mystery of the divine word, an artist skilled in his art, I know what belongs to it, the sinking waters, the weighing done for the reckoning of accounts, how to produce the forms of going forth and returning so that the limb may go to its place. I know the walking of the image of a man, the carriage of a woman, the two arms of Horus, the twelve circles . . . the poising of the arm to bring the hippopotamus low, the going of the runner. I know the making of amulets which enable us to go without the fire giving its flame on us, or the flood washing us away. . . ."[1] It is a curious medley of magic,

[1] Petrie I, p. 140, ll. 8–21.

mathematics, and art; but the architecture he produced, the pyramid and gorgeous temples attached to it, prove his mastery. They are covered with sculpture in low relief and coloured, which compares with the best work of Dynasty V.

The outstanding sovereign of this line was Mentuhotep II, who seems to have imposed himself as lord over his predecessor Intef III, who continued to rule under him. He ruled for forty-six years, and consolidated the Theban power so that his successors were able to develop it in many directions. Towards the close of his reign he sent his treasurer in charge of an expedition to the Wawat negroes to bring them under his sway, and this was the first move in a series of great adventures into the Sudan, which ended in its reduction under Sesostris II.

Another feature of his reign is the building of a temple in a new design of terraces so beautiful that it served as a model to the famous Queen Hatshepsut. His initiative in the south-east made possible to his successor, Senekhkere Mentuhotep III, an adventure on a larger scale, of which we have a full account written by the leader, Hennu. This shows how well the district was organized in town and country divisions, each under its own officer of the king's house; how the nomad tribes were employed in scouting and outpost work while the main body was held well together under a single command. The Egyptians were a naturally un-warlike folk and for such undertakings no doubt

the experiences of military rule during the disorders proved to have had their uses in teaching
the rulers tactical skill and care of supplies and
lines of communication. This development of the
route to the sea by well digging was most valuable
work by which coming kings were to profit greatly.

(Hennu's expedition to Punt :)[1] "My lord, life,
prosperity, health sent me to despatch a ship to
Punt to bring for him fresh myrrh from the sheiks
over the Red Land, by reason of the fear of him
in the highlands.

"Then I went forth from Koptos (Kuft) upon
the road, which his majesty commanded me.
There was with me an army of the South from [——]
of the Oxyrrhincus Nome, the beginning thereof
as far as Gebelen (*sic*), the end thereof as far as
[——], every officer of the king's house, those
who were in town and field, united, came after
me.

"The army cleared the way before, overthrowing
those hostile to the king, the hunters and the
children of the highlands were posted as the protection of my limbs. Every official body was
placed under my authority. They reported messengers to me, as one alone commanding to whom
many hearken.

"I went forth with an army of 3,000 men. I
made the road a river and the Red Land a stretch
of field, for I gave a leathern bottle, a carrying pole,
2 jars of water, and 20 loaves to each one among

[1] Br. I, p. 209, ll. 6-22.

them every day. The asses were laden with sandals. . . .

" Now I made 12 wells in the bush and 2 wells in Idehet 20 square cubits in one, and 31 square cubits in another in Iheteb 20 by 20 cubits on each side. . . .

" Then I reached the Red Sea ; then I made this ship, and I despatched it with everything. . . ."

At the end of the reign of Mentuhotep IV a great expedition was sent to the Hammamat quarries to establish regular quarters, and from the extraordinary powers entrusted to the leader, a certain Amenemhet, the king's vizier, it seems likely that he is the same as the Amenemhat who succeeds to the throne as founder of Dynasty XII.

CHAPTER V

THE TWELFTH DYNASTY (*circa* 2000 B.C.)

THE exact relation of this Dynasty to the
last is not yet clear, but the first of the line,
Amenemhet I, was certainly akin to Senekhkere. He did not succeed without one or two
vigorous campaigns, but it is not clear whether
these were waged against his predecessor or some
rival among the great feudal nobles, others of whom,
however, like Khnumhotep, to whom he granted
the Oryx Nome, evidently supported him. He was
a most capable, vigorous ruler, and is said to have
made a survey of the land and divided it afresh
into provinces—work which would be very needful
after the disorders. He drew up " Instructions "
for his son. In these he relates the danger he
incurred from a conspiracy at the close of his reign
and avows the bitterness it aroused in him, which
disgusted him with the rule, so that he installed
his son as heir and co-regent with himself. This
example was followed by other kings of the Theban
line and served to give security to the succession.
The story runs :[1]

[1] Br. I, pp. 231, 232.

" It was after the evening meal
I took an hour of heart's ease
Lying upon my couch, I relaxed ;
My heart began to follow slumber.
Behold weapons were flourished,
Council was held against me,
While I was like a serpent of the desert.
I awoke to fight utterly alone.
As I quickly grasped the weapons in my hand,
I hurled back the wretches,
Behold the abomination occurred while I was
      without thee,
While the Court had not yet heard,
That I had delivered to thee the kingdom,
While I had not yet sat with thee.
Let me adjust thy adminstration ;
For I do not terrify them, I do not think of them,
My heart does not endure the slackness of
      servants."

Later the poem gives a summary of the work
of the reign :
" I sent to Elephantine,
I reached the Delta,
I stood on the borders of the land,
I inspected its interior,
I carried forward the boundaries of valour, by
      my bravery, by my deeds,
I was one who cultivated grain, who loved the
      harvest god ;
The Nile greeted me in every valley ;

None was hungry in my years, none thirsted
    then ;
One dwelt at peace, through that which I did,
    conversing concerning me.
All that I commanded was correct.
I captured lions, I took crocodiles,
I seized the people of Wawat,
I captured the people of Mazoi.
I caused the Bedwin to go like hounds.
I made a palace decked with gold
Whose ceilings were of lazuli and the walls
    therein.
The doors were of copper,
The bolts were of bronze
Made for everlastingness,
At which eternity trembles."

It was largely through the loyalty of the family
of Khnumhotep that Amenemhet I was able to
re-establish order, and we can read the history of
this great vassal house on the tomb inscriptions
of its members at Beni Hasan, and see that they
had a court and regular administration modelled
on that of the White House ; for Amenemhet found
it necessary to leave the ancient royal city of
Thebes and move his court to the North, where
the power of the feudal lords still required his
presence and control. He ruled from a spot close
to Memphis, and the White Wall became, as of old,
the emblem of the central authority.

The nobles of Beni Hasan had their tombs

excavated in the limestone cliffs of the western
bank of the Nile, and so fully decorated that they
give clear illustrations of the life in their nome.
They had begun as rulers of a narrow strip of the
valley, which was known as " The Horizon of
Horus." The first of the family was Khnumhotep
appointed by Amenemhet I to be[1] " hereditary
prince, count, governor of the Eastern Highlands
in Menet Khufu. He (i.e. Pharaoh) established
the Southern landmark, perpetuating the Northern,
like the heavens ; he divided the Great River
along its middle ; its eastern side of the Horizon
of Horus was as far as the Eastern Highland ; at
the coming of his Majesty when he cast out evil ;
shining like Atum himself, when he restored that
which he found ruined ; that which a city had
taken from its neighbour ; while he caused city
to know its boundary with city ; establishing their
landmarks like the heavens, distinguishing their
waters according to that which was in the writings,
investigating according to that which was of old,
because he so greatly loved justice.

" Lo, he appointed him to be hereditary prince,
count, great Lord of the Oryx Nome. He established the landmarks : the southern on his boundary
as far as the Hara Nome ; his northern as far as
the Jackal Nome. He divided the Great River
along its middle : its waters, its fields, its trees,
its sand as far as the Western Highlands."

Here we have the two steps in the rise of

[1] Br. I, p. 283, l. 10.

ANCIENT CAUSEWAY LEADING TO THE TOMB OF AMENEMHET

Khnumhotep: first his post as ruler of Menet Khufu, the Horizon of Horus, secondly his promotion to the position of Nomarch of Oryx.

Such offices were not necessarily hereditary: thus we see his son Nakht holding Menet Khufu only, but his son Ameni ruling the Oryx Nome; while his daughter Beket was married to Nehri, " governor of the residence city," and perhaps also lord of the Hare Nome. A second Khnumhotep succeeded Nakht in Menet Khufu, and to him came a troop of the Bedwin Aamu bringing tribute, a scene well known among Egyptian paintings. He married Kheti, daughter of the Nomarch of the Jackal region, and his sons Nakht II and Khnumhotep III held the Jackal Nome and Menet Khufu; the latter is called " Keeper of the Door of the Highlands."

These men had evidently a certain claim to succeed to the family Nome, and since inheritance was through the daughter, marriage was an important political affair. Yet Amenemhet seems to have retained a determining power over their posts. Their rule, like his, was a beneficent one, for they take pride in loving justice and in increasing the output of the lands and people under them. Unrest however was not quite crushed; even at the death of Amenemhet I the presence of rivals for the throne seems to be suggested in the story of Sinuhe. The heir to the throne, Sesostris, and the prince, Sinuhe, were both with the army in Libya when news of the death of Pharaoh was brought to the

camp by a messenger. Sesostris hurried off at
once to Memphis, without announcing his departure.
Sinuhe was seized with panic fear, the reason of
which does not appear ; probably he was either
guilty of conspiracy or expected to be falsely
charged with it.   We have from his own mouth the
story of his adventures.[1]

"Behold I stood ; I heard his voice (i.e. the
        messenger's)
As he spoke. . . .
My heart clave, my arms opened,
While trembling fell on all my members.
I stole away
To seek for myself a place of concealment.
I placed myself between two bushes,
To avoid the way which they went.
I proceeded upstream
Not intending to reach the Court,
I thought there was fighting.

"I arrived at the Isle of Snefru (possibly the
        Northern Isle).
I tarried in a stretch of field,
It grew light, I went on when it was day.
I came upon a man, standing in the way,
He saluted me and was afraid.
When the time of the evening meal drew on,
I reached the city of the Ox.
I ferried over in a vessel without a rudder,
(by means of) a wind of the West.

[1] Br. I, p. 236-9.

I passed by on the east of the quarry,
Past the Highland goddess, mistress of the Red
    Mountain,
As I gave the way to my feet going northward
I came to the walls of the Ruler,
Made to repulse the Bedwin,
And to smite the Sandrangers
I bowed down in the bushes,
For fear the sentinels on the fort
Who belonged to its day [-watch] should see me.
I went on at time of evening,
As the earth brightened I arrived at Peten.
When I had reached the lake of Kemwer (' the
    Great Black,' the northern extension of
    the Gulf of Suez)
I fell down for thirst, fast came my breath,
My throat was hot,
I said ' This is the taste of death.'
I upheld my heart, I drew my limbs together,
As I heard the sound of the lowing of cattle,
I beheld the Bedwin.
That chief among them, who had been in Egypt,
    recognized me.
He gave me water, he cooked for me milk.
I went with him to his tribe.
Good was that which they did.
One land sent me on to another,
I loosed for Suan (a trading post on the Asiatic
    frontier),
I arrived at Kedem ;
I spent a year and a half there.

Emuienshi, that sheik of Upper Tenu (Upper
    Retenu, Highlands of Palestine) brought
    me forth
Saying to me ' Happy art thou with me. . . .
Behold, thou shalt now abide with me ;
Good is that which I shall do for thee.'
He put me at the head of his children,
He married me to his eldest daughter,
He made me select for myself of his land,
Of the choicest of that which he had,
On his boundary with another land.
It was a goodly land named Yaa.
There were figs in it and vines,
More plentiful than water was its wine,
Copious was its honey, plenteous its oil ;
All fruits were upon its trees.
Barley was there and spelt
Without end all cattle.

I spent many years,
My children became strong,
Each the mighty man of his tribe,
The messenger going north,
Or passing southward to the Court (Court of
    Egypt),
He turned in to me.
For I had all men turn in.''

Sinuhe remained in Palestine to a good old age,
but then a great home-sickness came upon him
and he wrote a pathetic appeal to the Pharaoh

for pardon and leave to return to end his days in
Egypt.[1]

" Let this flight obtain thy forgiveness,
That I may be appointed in the Palace,
That I may see the place where my heart dwells.
How great a thing is it
That my body may be embalmed in the land
    where I was born !
To return here is happiness."

Sesostris replied to this appeal :

" Leave all the riches that thou hast
And that are with thee, altogether.
When thou shalt come into Egypt, behold ! the
    Palace ;
When thou shalt enter the Palace, bow thy face
    to the ground
Before the Great House ;
Thou shalt be chief among the Companions.
And day by day behold ! thou growest old ;
Thy vigour is lost ;
And thou thinkest on the day of burial.
Thou shalt see thyself come to the blessed state ;
They shall give thee bandages from the hand of
    Tait,
(on) The night of applying the oil of embalming.
They shall follow thy funeral,
And visit the tomb on the day of burial,

[1] Petrie I, p. 154-5.

Which shall be in a gilded case,
The head painted with blue,
A canopy of cypress-wood above thee,
And oxen shall draw thee,
The singers going before thee,
And they shall dance the funeral dance,
The weepers crouching at the door of thy tomb
Shall cry aloud the prayers for offerings ;
They shall slay victims for thee at the door of
      thy pit ;
And thy pyramid shall be carved in white stone,
In the company of the royal children.
Thus thou shalt not die in a strange land.
Nor be buried by the Aamu ;
Thou shalt not be laid in a sheepskin when thou
      art buried ;
All people shall beat the earth and lament on
      thy body
When thou goest to the tomb."

Sinuhe, on receiving this sympathetic message,
at once disposes himself to leave Palestine. He
makes a feast and instals his son as chief in his place,
making over his goods, people, and lands to him.
At the frontier fort he is received by royal officers
with supplies ; he there dismisses his Semite following and goes with the four messengers to the
court. The Queen and family do not, naturally,
recognize him, but he is given an establishment.
" He cast away his foreign dress, shaved his long
hair, wore fine linen and slept on a bedstead," and

so, resuming all the manners of his youth, ended his days in peace, reconciled to Sesostris.

The poem is of great value historically, giving as it does in detail the first clear picture of an intercourse between Egypt and Palestine which must have been long current, for Sinuhe speaks of the messengers passing north and south between Egypt and Syria as of a regular service, and seems himself to have some authority over this traffic : " For I had all men (passing or trafficking like the Midianite merchantmen of a later date) to turn in." Like the scenes from the Old Testament and the later tales of Wenamon, this poem opens a priceless glimpse into the early life of Syrian peoples, among whom " Abraham " might then be numbered, about 1950 B.C.

The intercourse between Egypt and Syria is further shown by the visit of a body of Aamu or Semites to the court of Khnumhotep II at Menet-Khufu. They are shown wearing long, straight dresses, curiously and richly embroidered, and bringing with them offerings of deer and of a cosmetic for painting the eyelids.

Sesostris, or Usertsen I, whose accession and secure reign are inferred in the story of Sinuhe, was the prince who had already aided his father in governing after the conspiracy against his life had disenchanted him. At the close of the old king's reign the prince seems to have led an adventure into Nubia, feeling his way into the country formed by the Nile's westward turn, and the

5

country of the Wawat, and coming into hostile touch with the Mazoi, or Matchai. Punitive assaults were made too on " the Troglodytes, the Asiatics, and Sand-dwellers," the roving mixed tribes of the eastern highlands between Red Sea and Nile, and a fort was garrisoned to prevent their descents.

The work thus begun he carried forward with great vigour when reigning, and almost at once led a large force in person into Kush, where dwelt the Isthet, Sethu, and Mazoi. This seems to have overawed them into submission, for the Egyptians suffered no loss. By his eighth year Sesostris was able to send a second force under a commander, Mentuhotep, who reached the point known now as Wadi Halfa, and there erected a slab bearing the names of ten districts which had yielded to him. He seems to have presumed on this success, for his name has been erased and he appears no more. The object of these conquests seems to have been the hunt for treasure ; and from now on the gold of Nubia forms a recognized part of the state's resources. On the west, too, Sesostris opened intercourse of an official kind with the oases.

The activity of the Pharaohs of Dynasty XII was marked. The expeditions made by Sesostris I were repeated under Amenemhet II, an officer named Sihathor leading them to Sinai and to Nubia. His record says : [1]

" I visited the mine-land as a youth, and I forced

[1] Br. I, pp. 274-5.

the (Nubian) chiefs to wash gold. I brought malachite (a mineral much used to make a green inlay). I reached Nubia of the negroes. I went overthrowing by the fear of the Lord of the Two Lands. I came to He (i.e. Semreh), I went around its islands, I brought away its produce . . . Sihathor triumphant."

Another officer took an army by sea to Punt, and reported " his arrival in safety from Punt ; his army being with him, prosperous and healthy ; and his ships having made land at Sewew."

Under the next Pharaoh, Sesostris II, great attention was paid to Punt and to Red Sea trade generally. Intercourse was frequent also with Syria, as it has been seen to be already under Sesostris I in the story of Sinuhe ; yet it hardly seems to be sufficient to bear out the statement of Manetho, " He conquered all Asia in nine years."

These Theban Pharaohs were not builders of great pyramids, and their buildings were mainly of brick only, cased with stone.

A pecular pyramid was cut and built by Sesostris II out of a great outcrop of rock at Il-lahun. By cutting away parts the solid rock itself was fitted to make part of the walls, and to this granite and brickwork were added, and beside it grew up a temporary town for the workmen, covering an area of over eighteen acres. It has been recently discovered, and is found to contain great houses for the officials in charge, and rows and rows of small huts for the workmen—over 2,000 rooms.

The place seems to have been abandoned gradually, and its rooms contain much of valuable evidence of the life of the time amongst the rubbish its people threw into some abandoned cottages. Sesostris II did good work in organizing the new province of the Fayum, the rich oasis area. He was followed by Sesostris III, an arrogant, powerful prince. The main work of his reign was the conquest and subjection of the Sudan. There seem to have been three expeditions in the eighth, twelfth, and sixteenth years of his reign. The old canals cut at the first cataract by Uni seem to have disappeared, but one cut in the first year of his reign was cleared out and used in the eighth year. " His majesty commanded to make the canal anew, the name of this canal being ' Beautiful are the ways of Kekure (Sesostris) Living Forever,' when his majesty proceeded up river to overthrow Kush, the wretched."[1]

On later occasions Sesostris caused stone steles to be set up as boundary pillars at Semneh between Egypt and the Sudan, on one is this inscription :[2] " Southern boundary, made in the year 8, under the majesty of the king of Upper and Lower Egypt, Kekure, who is given life for ever and ever ; in order to prevent that any Negro should cross it, by water or by land, with a ship or any herds of the Negroes ; except a Negro who shall come to do trading in Iken (not identified) or with a commission. Every good thing shall be done with them,

[1] Br. I, p. 292, ll. 9–11.   [2] Br. I, p. 293.

but without allowing a ship of the Negroes to pass by Heh (Semneh) going downstream for ever."

On a second monument is this :[1] " Year 16, third month of the second season occurred his majesty's making the southern boundary as far as Heh. I have made my boundary beyond that of my fathers : I have increased that which was bequeathed to me. I am a king who speaks and executes ; that which my heart conceives is that which comes to pass by my hand . . . eager to possess . . . not allowing a matter to sleep in his heart . . . attacking him who attacks, silent in a matter, or answering a matter according to that which is in it, since if one is silent after attack, it strengthens the heart of the enemy. Valiance is eagerness, cowardice is to slink back ; he is truly a craven who is repelled upon his border ; since the Negro hearkens to the [――] of the mouth ; it is answering him which drives him back ; when one is eager against him, he turns his back ; when one slinks back he begins to be eager. But they are not a people of might, they are poor and broken in heart. My majesty has seen them, it is not an untruth.

" I captured their women, I carried off their subjects, went forth to their wells, smote their bulls ; I reaped their grain, and set fire thereto. As my father lives for me, I speak in truth, without a lie therein coming out of my mouth. Now as for every son of mine who shall maintain this boundary

[1] Br. I, p. 295-6.

which my majesty has made, he is my son, he is born to my majesty, the likeness of a son who is the champion of his father, who maintains the boundary of him that begat him. Now as for him who shall relax it, and shall not fight for it ; he is not my son, he is not born to me."

The main object of this conquest was still treasure hunting. Nubia was a land of gold, and Sesostris required much fine gold, both for trading and decorative purposes. He built and repaired temples and made a new figure of the god Osiris, and a new boat for it, for the ceremonies and miracle play of this god's story were steadily growing in importance and elaboration.

An interesting scene from the reign of Sesostris III is preserved on the tomb-inscription of Thuthotep. Prince of the Hare Nome, who was able to employ four ranks of subjects to do the work of hauling a great statue to adorn it. The description [1] says :

" Following is a statue of 13 cubits, of stone of Hatnub. Lo, the way upon which it came, was very difficult, beyond anything. Lo, the dragging of the great things was difficult for the heart of the people, because of the difficult stone of the ground, being hard stone.

" I caused the youth, the young men of the recruits to come, in order to make for it a road, together with shifts of necropolis miners and of quarrymen, the foremen and the wise. The people of strength said ' We come to bring it ' ; while my

[1] Br. I, p. 310, ll. 8–24.

heart was glad ; the city was gathered together rejoicing ; very good it was to see beyond anything The old man among them, he leaned upon the child, the strong-armed together with the tremblers, their courage rose. Their arms grew strong ; one of them put forth the strength of a thousand men. . . . Behold, this statue, being a squared block on coming forth from the great mountain, was more valuable than anything. Vessels were equipped, filled with supplies, in advance of my army of recruits. . . . My nome shouted praise. I arrived in the district of this city, the people were gathered together, praising ; very good it was to see, beyond anything. . . ."

Such quarrying achievements were turned to different uses.

While pyramids cease to be built after the Theban period, these kings introduced two new features into Egyptian architecture : one the use of obelisks in connexion with their temples ; the other the multiplying of immense statues of themselves. Of these colossi some were forty or fifty feet high. There were ten such portraits of Amenemhet I, sixteen of Amenemhet II, and naturally what was gained in quantity was lost in quality, stereotyped patterns and rules were followed, and the living character of the man was buried under art convention.

Sesostris III made at least one raid into Syria, but with no permanent effect : " His majesty proceeded northward, to overthrow the Asiatics.

His majesty arrived at a district, Sekmem was its name. His majesty led the good way in proceeding to the palace of ' Life, Prosperity, and Health,' when Sekmem had fallen together with Retenu' the wretched, whilst I was acting as rear-guard.

" Then the citizens of the army mixed in, to fight with the Asiatics. Then I captured an Asiatic, and had his weapons seized by two citizens of the army, for one did not turn back from the fight, but my face was to the front, and I gave not my back to the Asiatic."[1]

The same somewhat boastful spirit pervades this record as that of the sovereign, whose influence would no doubt encourage it in his servants. The king's glory is the subject of a fine hymn, a copy of which written on papyrus was found at Kahun. Parts of it run :[2]

HYMN

I. " Twice joyful are the gods, thou hast estab-
        lished their offerings,
      Twice joyful are the princes, thou hast
        formed their boundaries.
      Twice joyful are thy ancestors before thee,
        thou hast increased their portions.
      Twice joyful is Egypt at thy strong arm,
        thou hast guarded the ancient order.
      Etc., etc.

[1] Br. I, pp. 304–5.   [2] Petrie I, p. 182.

II.   " Twice great are the owners of his city, for
        he is a multitude and an host.

      Twice great are the owners of his city, for
        he is a floodgate, pouring forth the
        streams of its waterfloods.

      Twice great are the owners of his city, for
        he is a bower letting every man lie down
        in the midday heat.

      Twice great are the owners of his city, for
        he is a screen like walls built of sharp
        stones of Ketem.

      Etc., etc.

III. " He has come to us, he has taken the land of
        the well, the double crown is placed on
        his head.

      He has come, he has united the Two Lands,
        he has joined the kingdom of the Upper
        Land with the Lower.

      He has come, he has ruled Egypt, he has
        placed the desert in his power.

      He has come, he has protected his frontier,
        he has rescued the robbed.

      " He has come, we bring up our children, we
        bury our aged by his good favour."

      Etc., etc.

Similar worship of the glory of the god king is
evidenced in the next reign by the writing of
Sehetepabra, a director of works at Abydos, who
says to his descendants :[1]

[1] Br. I, p. 327, ll. 1–28.

" Adore the king, Nematre (Amenemhet III)
     living forever in the midst of your bodies ;
Enthrone his majesty in your hearts. . . .
He is the sun, seeing with his rays. . . .
He makes the Two Lands green, more than a
     Great Nile. . . .
The king is food.
His mouth is increase.
He is the one creating that which is. . . .
The Begetter, who causes the people to be. . . .
Fight for his name,
Purify yourselves by his oath,
And ye shall be free from trouble.
The beloved of the king shall be blessed.
There is no tomb for one hostile to his majesty.
But his body shall be thrown to the waters."

AMENEMHET III

Amenemhet III seems to have reaped where his
father had sown, like Charlemagne and the Emperor
Otto I ; and, like our own king Henry VIII, he
inherited a well-established kingdom, and largely
owing to his father's achievements he attained fame
as the greatest Pharaoh of his line : " He reigned
at least 44 years, and Egypt under his rule enjoyed
great peace and prosperity.   Art, sculpture, architecture and trade of all kinds flourished."   Some
think that it was he who caused the Sphinx to be
made, but this is unlikely.   He did, however, build a
pyramid and a most elaborate temple near to it, which

the Greeks called the Labyrinth, probably 800,000 square feet in extent, the large chambers in it representing the various nomes and the small rooms particular towns. Pliny says that it contained figures of gods, statues of kings, and effigies of hideous monsters, and most of it was in total darkness ; it was dedicated to the ancient crocodile god Sebek. In reality this building was the State office for the management of lands reclaimed in the Fayum. This was due to the king's work in building a huge reservoir in the Fayum oasis, by increasing the size of a natural lake to 750 square miles. The water so reserved was used in the dry season, and was enough to double the weight of water on the Lower Nile for a hundred days. It was he, too, who measured the annual rise of the Nile waters by cutting marks on the rock at Semneh. These things would increase the fertility of the land and make farming more scientific. From his reign we have the record of an officer named Ptahwer, made in the " Year 45 under the majesty of the good god, Lord of the Two Lands, Nematre (Amenemhet III), given life forever, beloved of Hathor."

Ptahwer describes himself as " ready in his reports to his lord [delivering] Asia to him who is in the palace, bringing Sinai at his heels, traversing inaccessible valleys, bringing unknown extremities [of the world], the master of the double cabinet, chief of the Treasury, Ptahwer triumphant."[1]

[1] Br. I, p. 319, ll. 24–28.

Another officer was sent to search for fresh quarries, probably in the Wady Maghara, and gives a very human account of his difficulties with the workmen, who grumbled sadly at being sent at an unusual season of the year : " The majesty of this god (Amenemhet) despatched the treasurer of the god, master of the double cabinet—Harurre to this Mineland ; I arrived in this land in the third month of the second season although it was not the season for going to this Mineland. This treasurer of the god saith to the officials who shall come to this Mineland at this season : ' Let not your face flinch on that account ; behold, Hathor will turn it to profit.' I looked to myself and I dealt with myself ; when I came from Egypt my face flinched and it was hard for me. . . . The highlands are hot in summer, and the mountains brand the skin. When morning dawns a man is [——], I addressed the workmen concerning it : ' How favoured is he who is in this Mineland ! ' They said, ' There is malachite in this eternal mountain ; it is [——] to seek [it] at this season. One like us hears the like of [such] marvels coming at this season. It is [——] to [——] for it in this evil summer season.' [1]

" I succeeded in mining the good sort, and I finished in the first month of the third season. I brought genuine costly stone for the luxuries, more than anyone. . . . It was better than the accustomed seasons thereof. Offer ye, offer ye to the mistress of Heaven, appease ye Hathor ; if ye do it, it will be profitable for you. . . . I led my army very kindly, and I was not loud-voiced toward the workmen. I acted before all the army and the recruits they rejoiced in me ! . . ." [1]

The great increase in wealth and prosperity under this last great king of the Theban line did not prevent a sudden collapse of his house. Probably the great nobles had increased in power and wealth, possibly foreign influences were at work ; at any rate, Amenemhet III, having reigned for nearly fifty years, his son, Amenemhet IV, was no doubt elderly and reigned only nine years, associating with him in the government his sister Sebeknefrure, who outlived him and reigned alone for four years. This was the chance for rivals, and a different Dynasty XIII succeeded. After it came chaos.

[2] Br. I, p. 322, ll. 5-20.

CHAPTER VI

THE HYKSOS (*circa* 1700 B.C.)

THIS confused interlude in the due sequence of Egyptian sovereigns lasted some hundreds of years. Manetho calls it 1590 years, and mentions five different Dynasties from XIII to XVII, but his list does not agree with other known facts, or even with the length of the reigns which he mentions. All we can gather is that after Amenemhet III the power of the Theban kings rapidly dwindled, and at the same time Semite tribes worked their way into Egypt and acquired control of one district after another. Already these nomads had been trading with Egypt and befriending Egyptians under the Twelfth Dynasty, and it is natural that the wealth of the later reigns should have attracted them more and more. The Egyptians called them Hequ Shasu, chiefs, nomads, which was shortened into Hyksos, and expressed by the figure which appears to stand for mountain peaks, and so to indicate a people from " over the hills." Hyksos is usually rendered shepherd kings, and these were no doubt closely akin in habits and wealth to the patriarch chiefs like Jacob and Lot of whom the Old Testament gives us such intimate pictures. Another word used for them by the Egyptians is Aat-t, the pests or filthy ones, but Egypt was unable to repulse them. The Dynasty XIII were probably kings of Upper Egypt, while the Fourteenth ruled in the Delta, perhaps at the same time, and rivalry between them weakened the Two Lands. Yet Sekhemre-Khutowe was the first king of the Thirteenth Dynasty, and his records appear both at Bubastis in the Delta and among the Nile level measurements at Semneh, so that he must still have been recognized in both lands like the kings of Dynasty XII.

A later king, Neferhotep, seems to have usurped the throne of Upper Egypt, for his father was only a priest. A record tells how he visited the temple of Osiris at Abydos and the pains he took to restore the worship of this god, probably to strengthen his own position with priests and people :

" I am his (i.e. Osiris') son, his protector, he giveth to me the inheritance of the earth. (I) am the King, great in strength, excellent in commandment. He shall not live who is hostile to me : he shall not breathe the air who revolts against me ; his name shall not be among the living ; his KA shall be seized before the officials. . . ."[1]

These are not the phrases that an accepted king would use ; they certainly imply insecurity and the need for severe measures to maintain the sceptre.

[1] Br. I, p. 336.

Neferhotep reigned eleven years, and was a great king ruling from the Delta to the second cataract, but the power evidently lapsed at his death, for there followed a quick succession of kings, and many of them seem to have been no more than local lords.

A record probably belonging to the close of this period and to the reign of a petty king of Thebes, Nubkheprure-Intef, describes the fate ordained for a traitor :

" Behold there is brought to you this decree. . . . An evil thing is about to happen in this temple. Foes have been [stirred up] by, a curse to his name, Teti, son of Minhotep. Cause him to be deposed from the temple of my father, Min. Cause him to be cast out of his temple office, from son to son and heir to heir; [——] upon the earth ; take away his bread, his food and his joints of meat. His name shall not be remembered in this temple, according as it is done towards one like him, who is hostile towards the enemies of his god. His entries shall be cast out from the temple of Min, from the treasury and on every book likewise."[1]

The fullest account of the coming of the Hyksos is given by Flavius Josephus, who borrows from Manetho's history of Egypt. He says : " I will set down his very words, as if I were to bring the very man himself into court for a witness.

" There was a king of ours (i.e. Egyptian), whose

[1] Br. I, pp. 340-1.

name was Timaus. Under him it came to pass, I know not how, that God was averse to us, and there came, after a surprising manner, men of ignoble birth, out of the eastern parts, and had boldness enough to make an expedition into our country, and with ease subdued it by force, yet without our hazarding a battle with them.

" So when they had gotten those that governed us under their power, they afterwards burned down our cities, and demolished the temples of the gods, and used all the inhabitants after a most barbarous manner ; nay, some they slew, and led their children and their wives into slavery. At length they made one of themselves king, whose name was Salatis (i.e. Shalit, Semitic for Governor) ; he also lived in Memphis, and made both the Upper and Lower Lands pay tribute, and left garrisons in places that were most proper for them. He selected the city of Avaris on the Damietta arm of the Nile as his stronghold. He was succeeded by 5 other kings, who were all along making war with the Egyptians, and were very desirous gradually to destroy them to the very roots. The whole nation was styled Hyksos, that is ' Shepherd Kings.' . . . These people kept possession of Egypt 511 years."

Two names of their kings are known, Apep and Khian, the two last but one in Manetho's list (Apophis and Khian). The Hyksos adopted gradually the names, costume, and customs of the

6

Egyptian kings, used their language, and accepted
their religious beliefs and practices, calling themselves " Sons of Ra," though they did not abandon
their Syrian religion, the worship of Sutek (Set or
Baal). Yet in spite of their long rule the Hyksos
never became identified with their subjects, and
were at last overthrown by insurrections led by two
spirited princes of Thebes ; the first succeeded in
hemming them into Avaris, and the second besieged
and took the place. The Hyksos were allowed to
depart with all " their families and effects, in number
not less than 240,000, and bent their way through
the desert to Syria," they built " a city of sufficient
size to contain this multitude of men, and they
gave it the name of Jerusalem." Such is Josephus'
story of this earlier exodus of a Semite people, but
it is, he adds, an anachronism that the building
of Jerusalem was due to the fear in which the
Hyksos still stood of the great Assyrian power.
The period was about 2000 to 1600 B.C., a time
when the Israelites were making their first settlements in Palestine, and Assyria was only just
arising.

Josephus' account of the Hyksos must be checked
by any obtainable fragments of earlier references
to them, and though there are few, they suggest
some important differences. In the monuments
of the time of their overthrow they are called
" Asiatics "—barbarians ; and this may be taken
to confirm Manetho's description of them as
Phœnicians and Arabians. They were probably

descendants of some Semite emigration from Arabia into Palestine. The name is most likely a Greek form of the Egyptian title " Ruler of Countries," which is born on the inscriptions of a Hyksos king, Khian or Jaunes, of whom traces are also found as far from Egypt as Bagdad, Syria, and Knossos in Crete. Breasted suggests that a Semitic suzerainty may have existed from the Euphrates to the Isles of the Sea, having its principal seat at Kadesh, which would account for the placing of the Egyptian capital, Avaris, on the extreme north-east frontier of the Delta.

But the problem remains one worth infinite effort to unravel.

Egyptian princes seem to have maintained themselves in Thebes throughout the Hyksos period, and gradually to have regained strength for the final victorious rebellion. These Thebans are called Dynasty XVII. Their names were Sekenenre I, II, etc. The body of the third has been found with the skull split and jawbone broken and a stab from a dagger over the eye, and this gives a hint of the furious warfare through which the freedom of the land was regained. The two last kings of the line were brothers, and call themselves sons of the Moon, " born of Thoth." With the last of the family, Ahmose, the Eighteenth Dynasty begins, and the re-conquest is complete.

THE EMPIRE DYNASTY XVIII (1580 B.C.)

With the rise of this new Theban house and the expulsion of the Semites, several changes in the economic state of Egypt appear to have taken place. It differs completely from the earlier Theban rule in that it is free both in theory and practice from the disruptive feudalism which had been an ever-present danger to that Middle Kingdom.

The Hebrew account of Egypt (Gen. 47) attributes to Joseph the vital change, whereby the land of Egypt came to be called Pharaoh's own. Is there perhaps some germ of historic truth in this ? It may represent facts. It was the faction of local lords or rival kings which had made possible the peaceful penetration of Egypt by Semite strangers. When that immigration placed a stranger on the throne, his gradual conquest or subjugation of the land and his foreign ideas of lordship may have obliterated once for all in the North the old constitutional claims of the people. Further, the famine which must always follow prolonged warfare in hot countries, where the failure to cultivate at the right season involves complete loss of the crop, must have ensued, and no doubt the story of the Pharaoh's dream of the seven lean kine, and Joseph's interpretation, is a picturesque, popular rendering of the means taken by the highly civilized Semite power to provide by central administration

MODELS SHOWING PROCESS OF BEER-MAKING

against such a calamity. Perhaps as the British strangers tackled the vast famines of India, clever Hyksos devised means against those in the lands their irruptions had temporarily wasted. The result, bringing every field of Egypt into the hand of the Pharaoh's officer, could not but strike deep into the people's imagination, and would naturally give birth to some such version of the causes. In one detail at least the Biblical story gives strictly historical fact : the one exception to this general escheat of Egyptian lands to the crown was the great one of the land of the priests. Each temple had not only its surrounding area but large distant estates from which it drew supplies. To what an extent this became the case appears in the Twentieth and Twenty-first Dynasties, when Amon-Re possessed nearly a third of the territory of Egypt. The concentration of land in Pharaoh's hand, and the theory that all land was his, made impossible any hereditary gifts of districts from ruler to son without Pharaoh's sanction ; it made possible to the Crown a complete system of taxation, one-fifth being the legal due from all landholders—a claim moderate for the East ; civil labour and military service would also become his right, and all these powers made possible the rise of a Dynasty to imperial height.

How much of the framework of such an organization was due in the Eighteenth Dynasty to the overthrown Hyksos rule it would be rash to guess, but the condition of the cities and lands, like

Phœnicia and the seaport towns of the Levant, and those on the Orontes valley, shows clearly, if scholars are right in looking on these as fragments of their empire, that theirs was a progressive, highly developed civilization.

The first fifteen years of the reign of Ahmose I (Amosis) were spent in battling with the Hyksos and driving out the last of them, whom he followed up into Palestine.   Records of this fighting remain from the tombs of two great officers, both of the famous family ruling at Nekheb, and both named Ahmose like the king : Ahmose, son of (the lady) Ebana and Ahmose Pen-nekhbet.

The son of Ebana relates his early career :[1] " I spent my youth in the city of Nekheb, my father being an officer of the king of Upper and Lower Egypt, Sekenenre, triumphant, Baba, son of Royenet, was his name.   Then I served as an officer in his stead, in the ship ' The Offering ' . . . while I was still young, not having taken a wife and while I was still sleeping in the [——] garment." Here we have the old loyal family of the rulers of Nekheb doing regular naval service under the Sekenenre house, which seems to corroborate a picture of the conditions given in a later folk-story told in the days of the Rameses Pharaohs. The tale goes that a messenger came to Sekenenre from Apophis—his Hyksos overlord in the city of Avaris—to Thebes to complain that the emperor could not sleep in his Delta capital for the clamour

[1] Br. II, p. 6.

of the hippopotami in the pool at Thebes, some 400 miles away. The vassal-king was speechless at such an outrageous pretext for war, but he " caused to summon his great princes, likewise his officers and leaders," and though they were as aghast as himself they undoubtedly took action in a revolt which led to the overthrow of Apophis and all his race.

After serving thus in the local fleet in Nubia, Ahmose, son of Ebana, received the promotion of close attendance on the king in the war of liberty. " Then after I set up a household, I was transferred to the Northern Fleet, because of my valour, I followed the king on foot when he rode abroad in his chariot."

Ahmose I had now followed up the Hyksos to their northern stronghold and was about to deal the decisive blow, after a severe and prolonged struggle.

" The city of Avaris was besieged ; I showed valour on foot before his majesty ; then I was appointed to (the ship) ' Shining-in-Memphis.' There was fighting on the water in the canal : ' Pezedku of Avaris.' Then I fought hand to hand, I brought away a hand. (Hands were taken as trophies and counted.) It was reported to the royal herald. The gold of valour was given to me.

" Then there was again fighting in this place ; I again fought hand to hand there ; I brought away a hand. The gold of bravery was given to

me in the second place."[1]   Still Avaris held out,
and now an outbreak in far Southern Egypt calls
off the king and his loyal men of Nekheb to crush it.

" There was fighting in this Egypt, south of this
city (Nekheb) ; then I brought away a living
captive, a man ; I descended into the water, behold
he was brought as a seizure upon the road of this
city, I crossed with him over the water.   It was
announced to the royal herald.   Then I was
presented with gold in double measure."

This was a last effort of the local nobles to re-
assert themselves against Pharaoh, and no doubt the
influence of Ahmose of Nekheb in the district was
one reason of his accompanying the king.   This
danger crushed, Ahmose I was once more free for
the great work in the North.   The decisive campaign followed : " Avaris was captured," says the
general—no more ; but that was the turning-point
for the nation.   His own exploits are added : " I
took captive there one man and three women,
total four heads ;   his majesty gave them to me for
slaves."   The victory was followed up by a pursuit
into Palestine, for Ahmose says that in the king's
fifth year he took Sheruhen, a town later enumerated
in the allotment of towns to the twelve tribes.
There Ahmose took captive " two women and one
hand," and was rewarded with decoration as well
as with the captives.

King Ahmose I had wrought his country's
deliverance and might have hoped for peace, but

[1] Br. II, p. 7.

helped him to rally popular support; for the Hyksos had cruelly destroyed the Egyptian sanctuaries, overthrowing the best work of the Eleventh and Twelfth Dynasties and the mortuary monuments of the nobles as well as the kings. In his long reign of twenty-five years Ahmose had time after his wars to set about the restoration of the monuments. He reopened the great Turah quarries, and employed the labour of his captives as well as of his own people in rebuilding temples and monuments. In this work he was followed by his son Amenhotep I (Amenophis I), who was freed by his father's wars from any need of great military undertakings. He did, however, make an ascent into Nubia, and pushed forward the frontier after defeating a Nubian leader, with the aid of the two Ahmose. The son of Ebana, now an old man, relates his work in command of the fleet and army : [1]

" I sailed the king (Amenhotep I) triumphant, when he ascended the river to Kush, in order to extend the borders of Egypt. His majesty captured that Nubian Troglodyte in the midst of his army . . . who were brought away prisoners, none of them missing . . . thrust aside like those who are annihilated. Meanwhile I was at the head of our army; I fought incredibly; his majesty beheld my bravery. I brought off two hands, and took them to his majesty. One (i.e. Pharaoh) pursued his people and his cattle. Then I brought off a living prisoner, and took (him) to his majesty.

[1] Br. II, p. 17, l. 13–23.

" I brought his majesty in two days to Egypt
from the Upper Well (i.e. second cataract) ; I was
presented with gold." The distance is about 200
miles, this work therefore deserved recognition.
" Then I brought away two female slaves, in
addition to those which I had taken to his majesty.
One appointed me ' Warrior of the Ruler.' "

This campaign enabled Amenhotep thoroughly to
organize and settle Nubia as a district province,
under the charge of Nekhen as capital city. Its
chief magistrate, Harmini, administered it, collecting its tribute annually, much as an English sheriff
in Angevin times got in the king's dues, taking it
up to the Treasury at the White Wall and getting
his quittance. He states : " I passed many years
as mayor of Nekhen. I brought in its tribute to
the Lord of the Two Lands. . . . I attained
old age in Wawat. . . . I went north with its
tribute for the king each year ; I came forth thence
justified ; there was not found a balance against
me."[1]

Although no record of it remains, some campaign must have been waged by Amenhotep against
the remaining Hyksos power beyond his north-east
frontier, for his successor claims to rule as far as
the Euphrates, and makes this claim in his second
year, when he had certainly not himself made
such a conquest. To do so Amenhotep I must
have dealt with the power of Kadesh, which was a
flourishing place during the rule of Thutmose III,

[1] Br. II, p. 21, ll. 15-20.

and it is therefore probable that he did no more than mask the city and make a hurried raid into the Naharina. Even this would be an astonishing achievement and it is strange that no records of it should exist.

CHAPTER VII

THE EMPIRE: THUTMOSE I AND HAT-SHEPSUT

THUTMOSE I, who succeeded Amenhotep and built upon the solid foundation he had laid, was the heir by virtue of his marriage with the princess Ahmose rather than by birth; and through his mother's lower rank a fresh infusion of vigorous life seems to have entered the royal stock. The race was ripe for a great adventure, full of the stimulus of its recovered freedom, and in Thutmose I it found its fitting leader.

His first undertaking was in support of a newly created officer, the Viceroy of Kush, the region south of Nubia, between the second and fourth cataracts; the titles bestowed upon him were " Governor of the South, King's son of Kush "— the latter merely a title of honour, not a real relationship.

Kush was still a border province, not more completely controlled than our north-west frontier in India; its chiefs recognized only the strong hand and made constant raids from their fastnesses upon the settled points along the river, until

Pharaoh came up upon them with his fleet and
despatched their chief with his own hand. The
restless desert tribes were also handled, and the
whole of Southern Egypt, Nubia, and Kush
thoroughly pacified and organized under the
Viceroy Thure. The account of his great deeds
is recited in his third year in a Hymn of Victory,
engraved on the rocks on the island of Tombos,
just above the third cataract :[1]

" He hath taken his inheritance, he hath assumed
the seat of Horus . . . in order to extend the
boundaries of Thebes . . . so that the Sand-
dwellers and the barbarians shall labour for her
(i.e. Thebes). An abomination of the god are the
Haunebu ; bound are the Ekbet ; the Southerners
come down river, the Northerners come up river,
and all lands are together bringing their tribute
to the Good God, the primordial (Thutmose I). . . .
The [Sand]dwellers, chiefs of their tribes come to
him, bowing down ; the [interior] peoples send
to his majesty, doing obeisance to that which is
on his front (i.e. the sacred uraeus serpent).

" He hath overthrown the chief of the [Nubians] ;
the Negro is helpless, defenceless in his grasp. He
hath united the boundaries of his two sides (banks),
there is not a remnant among the curly-haired,
who come to attack him ; there is not a single
survivor among them. . . ."

The lords of the palace have made a fortress for
his army. " None faces him among the Nine

[1] Br. II, p. 29, ll. 16–23 ; p. 30, ll. 1–7.

Bows together ; like a young panther among the fleeing cattle ; the fame of his majesty blinded them." This fortress was to control the province now known as Dongola. " He brought the ends of the earth into his domain ; trod its two extremities with his mighty sword, seeking battle ; he found no one who faced him. He penetrated valleys which the ancestors knew not, which the wearers of the double diadem had not seen. His southern boundary is as far as the frontier of this land, his northern as far as that inverted water which goes downstream in going upstream (Euphrates River), subject to him are the isles of the Great Circle (ocean), the entire earth is under his feet. . . ."

Ahmose was with this king too as a fighting admiral : [1] " I sailed the king (Thutmose I) triumphant, when he ascended the river to Khenthennofer in order to cast out violence in the highlands, in order to suppress the raiding of the hill region. I showed bravery in his presence in the bad water, in the passage of the ship by the bend. I was appointed chief of the sailors. . . .

" His majesty was furious thereat (reason not given), like a panther ; his majesty cast his first lance, which remained in the body of that fallen one . . . powerless before his flaming uraeus, made [so] in an instant of destruction ; their people were brought off as living prisoners. His majesty sailed down river, with all countries in his grasp, that wretched Nubian Troglodyte being hanged head-

[1] Br. II, p. 33, l. 26.

downward, at the [prow] of the barge of his majesty,
and landed at Karnak."

On this Nubian expedition Thutmose cleared out
the canal at the first cataract, which had become
blocked with stone, so that on his way up it had
caused grave risks to the fleet, and Ahmose had
been proud of steering Pharaoh in safety " in the
bad water, in the passage of the ship by the bend."
Thus the king made good his line of communications
with the extreme south, so that trade as well as
naval traffic could be swift and safe.

" His majesty commanded to dig this canal, after
he found it [stopped up] with stones [so that] no
[ship sailed upon it].   [He sailed downstream] upon
it, his heart [glad, having slain his enemies]. . . .
His majesty sailed this canal in victory and power,
at his return from overthrowing the wretched Kush."[1]

The second great enterprise of Thutmose was
to bring in " the Northerners " by carrying war
into the highlands of Palestine and Syria and " the
land of the Two Rivers," the valley of the Tigris
and Euphrates.   The Hyksos' power still threatened
Egypt through these lands.   Ahmose writes :
" After these things (the king) journeyed to Retenu
to wash his heart (i.e. take vengeance) among the
foreign countries.   His majesty arrived at Naharin,
his majesty found that foe when he was [planning]
destruction ; his majesty made a great slaughter
among them.   Numberless were the living prisoners,
which his majesty brought off from his victories.

[1] Br. II, p. 32, ll. 7-10, 16.

7

" Meanwhile I was at the head of our troops, and his majesty beheld my bravery. I brought off a chariot, its horses, and him who was upon it as a living prisoner and took them to his majesty."[1]

Ahmose notes with satisfaction the capture of a chariot and horses, for these were the typical military unit of the Asiatic enemy and had been unknown in Egypt before the Hyksos' penetration. Henceforth they were to be typical of Egypt, and the desert-bred horse has become so much a feature there that it is hard to imagine a time when Egypt was horseless. This regular use of the horse by the Hyksos is another point hinting at Arabia as their original home. It is clear, from the reliefs illustrating Egyptian history from this time on, that the Egyptians had little difficulty in adopting the chariot. In the Twenty-first Dynasty they supply chariots and horses to Solomon (1 Kings x, 28, 29), and the Jews trade them to the northern Syrians and Hittites at a fixed rate. Save in the Greek work on the Parthenon there are few sculptured figures of horses more instinct with life and pace than those in the reliefs which describe the Egyptian campaigns in Palestine and Syria.

The reign of Thutmose I was a long one of thirty years, but its close is shrouded in a confused period of rivalry. Of his four children by Ahmose, the Theban lady, only one survived, and she a daughter, Hatshepsut.

There was prejudice in Egypt, stronger than any

[1] Br. II, p. 34, 35.

WOODEN MODEL—THE MAKING OF BEER

Salic law, against the rule of a woman, in spite of
the fact that inheritance went to the daughter and
not the son.   But Thutmose was determined to
retain the kingship in the due line of the Theban
kings, and hoped no doubt to avoid civil strife
by securing her succession.   She was therefore
acclaimed as his heir about the fifteenth year of
his reign.   Yet a man was on the throne even
before the death of Thutmose I—the prince named
Thutmose III—who had no claim except through
his father, unless he had formally espoused Hatshepsut, and could claim through her.   He had,
however, the support of the priesthood of Amon,
now at the height of their power.   He was himself
of their number and on May 3, 1501, was suddenly
proclaimed king by the image of the god itself
stopping abruptly before him as its procession made
the circuit of the temple hall, while Thutmose I,
his father, was performing the royal function of
sacrifice to the god.

For a time Thutmose III held the reins of government in his own hands, while his father and Hatshepsut retained secondary places.   But gradually
the party of the queen got the upper hand, so that
he was forced to place her beside him, first as
co-regent and finally as " king," so that she superseded him as the real ruler of Egypt.

The records relate :[1] " When he (Thutmose II)
went to heaven and was united with the gods, his
son stood upon his throne as king of Egypt, and he

[1] Budge, p.77, ll. 5–11.

ruled upon the throne of him that begot him. And his sister Hatshepsut was made a ruler of the country, and Egypt was under her jurisdiction, and Kamt (Egypt) performed for her works of service with due submission." Since Dynasty IV the theory was taught that every sovereign of Egypt was begotten of the god Amon-Re, and this story had now to be adapt·d to the rule of a queen. The legend was insisted upon in order to silence all questions of her authority, and it is elaborately and most beautifully told on a series of reliefs sculptured on a colonnade of her temple at Der-el-Bahri, and again at Luxor, and is written on a papyrus still existing, and known as the " Papyrus Westcar."

In the course of the legend the god Amon says to her mother, Queen Ahmose :[1] " Khnemet-Amon-Hatshepsut shall be the name of this my daughter . . . she shall exercise the excellent kingship in this whole land. My soul is hers, my bounty is hers, my crown is hers, that she may rule the Two Lands, that she may lead all the living. . . ."

In all the monuments of Hatshepsut there is such a mingling of religious myth and worship with historical fact that it seems to indicate a close alliance between the queen and the priesthood of Amon. The attribution of her origin to him, the use of his name for her, suggest this. In the record of her coronation Thutmose I is made to say in the person of Amon, " This is my daughter, Khnemet-Amon, Hatshepsut. . . . She is my successor upon

[1] Br. II, p. 80, ll. 23–26.

my throne. . . .   For thou art divine, O, daughter
of a god, for whom even the gods fight ; behind
whom they exert their protection every day according to the command of her father, the lord of the
gods."[1] Under this thin veil it is easy to see the
protection of the priesthood, and the queen's
ascendancy no doubt brought to it a more complete
influence in politics than before. Thutmose III,
as his later reign shows, was essentially a man of
war and it is perhaps natural that the priestly
party in thus forsaking his cause for that of
Hatshepsut, turned the resources of the state
towards works of peace. Directly she assumed the
power Hatshepsut began to build her temple at
Der-el-Bahri, entrusting the work to a sculptor,
loyal to herself, named Senmut.

This curious dual reign had lasted five years
when it was interrupted by that of Thutmose II,
another son of the old king Thutmose I, by the
princess Mutnofret, who was not of the Theban line.

It is possible that rumours of rebellion in Nubia
led to a demand for a man to lead the armies, or
it may be that the family differences had made
such a rising inevitable. In any case, news that
the Nine Bows were once more on the warpath
reached Thutmose II as he mounted the throne.
He at once despatched a force which had no difficulty
in reaching the third cataract and punishing the
marauders, capturing the chief's son and other
hostages. In Syria knowledge of the state of the

[1] Br. II, p. 97, l. 6.

Theban court would be quickly spread, and so it was that Thutmose I and II, who were ruling jointly, had to carry war as far as Niy on the Euphrates, punishing Bedouin rebels on the way ; and in this campaign Ahmose Pen-nekhbet fought his last fight. But this military revival was a short one. Thutmose I was aged and Thutmose II, as his mummy proves, was a prey to disease ; probably the death of the old king left the son too weak for conflict, and he made terms with his half-brother and for a time joined him as co-regent. But before long he died, and Thutmose III was once more overshadowed by his able queen, who now turned all her powers to the religious and peaceable ends she had had in view. " I have given thee all lands and all countries," says Amon-Re. " I conciliated them by love. (I), thy father, who sets thy fear among the Nine Bows, while they come in peace to all gods." And the queen herself makes claim not to conquest but to discovery and gain of wealth.

" I am adding increase to that which was formerly done ; to explore his (Amon's) ways, to learn his circuit, to open his highways."[1] " I have made bright the truth which he loved." " Punt is mine, and the fields of sycamore bearing fresh myrrh, the highways which were closed up and the two ways."

This lady, the first famous queen of whom history as yet can tell us, was very active in building and restoring temples to the gods. On the front of the cliff-temple of the eastern goddess, Pakht, she

[1] Br. II, pp. 120, 123.

gives an account of her work : " I have restored
that which was in ruins, I have raised up that which
was unfinished since the Asiatics were in the midst
of Avaris of the Northland, and the barbarians
were in the midst of them, overthrowing that which
was made, while they ruled in ignorance of Re."[1]

In this restoration of the worship of her father,
Amon-Re, Hatshepsut was led into far-reaching
expeditions. In the same inscription she says :
" The altars are opened, the sanctuaries are en-
larged. . . . I have made bright the truth, I eat
of its brightness . . . the lands together are under
my authority, the Black (South) and the Red
(Delta) are under my authority. . . . The land of
Reshu and the land of Yu, they cannot hide from
my majesty ; Punt is mine, and the fields of
sycamore bearing fresh myrrh."[2] Elsewhere she
says : " I have made for him a Punt in his garden,
just as he commanded me for Thebes. It is large
for him, he walks abroad in it."

It was this desire to perfect her cliff-temple to
Amon which instigated her greatest achievement,
the expedition to Punt. This temple was modelled
on the little temple of Mentuhotep II, and was built
in colonnades on terraces cut at the foot of the
cliff. This was the first use of columns to form a
colonnade and from it no doubt the Greeks borrowed
the idea of the pillared temples they afterwards per-
fected in the Parthenon and many other examples.

The story of the expedition is shown in the temple

[1] Br. II, p. 125.   [2] Br. II, pp. 123-4.

carvings. Ships are seen, first sailing the Red Sea and then the Nile, so that it seems possible that the canal connecting these by the Wadi Tumuli had already been cut. Hatshepsut appears as a man in royal dress and five vessels are shown getting under way.

Then comes the scene in Punt : the king's messenger with necklaces, hatchets, daggers, etc., is prepared to start trade with the Puntites. Their chief, Perehu, comes to meet him, followed by his grossly fat wife, Eti riding an ass, two sons and a daughter. The picture shows the pile-dwellings of the people of Punt built not far from the shore and backed by trees. They greet the Egyptians with questions : " Why have ye come hither unto this land which the people (of Egypt) know not ? Did ye come down upon the ways of heaven, or did ye sail upon the waters, upon the sea of God's Land ? Have ye trodden Re ? (i.e. come in the sky ?). Lo as for the King of Egypt, is there no way to His Majesty, that we may live by the breath which he gives ? "[1]

The men of Egypt then pitch a tent " in the myrrh-terraces of Punt by the side of the sea " and traffic. Two vessels are shown in the carving, heavily laden with myrrh-trees, ivory, apes, etc., with their gangways out and men busy going up and down with more trees and sacks of goods ; over them is written :[2]

" The loading of the ships very heavily with

[1] Br. II, p. 107.　　　[2] Br. II, p. 109.

marvels of the country of Punt ; all goodly, fragrant woods of God's Land, heaps of myrrh-resin, with fresh myrrh-trees, with ebony and pure ivory, with green gold of Emu, with cinnamon wood, khesyt wood, with ihmut-incense, sonter-incense, eye-cosmetic, with apes, monkeys, dogs, and the skins of the southern panther, with natives and their children." And over the men carrying trees from the forest is written : " Look to your feet, ye people ! Behold ! the load is very heavy ! Prosperity be with us, for the sake of the myrrh-tree in the midst of God's Land, for the house of Amon ; there is the place where it shall be made to grow for Makere, in his temple according to command." Another inscription says : " I (Makere, i.e. Hatshepsut) have made for him (Amon) a Punt in his garden, just as he commanded me, for Thebes. It is large for him, he walks abroad in it " ; and " Trees were taken up in God's Land and set in the ground in [Egypt]—for the king of the gods "[1]

The date of Queen Hatshepsut's death is not known but her husband survived her for many years, and during his sole reign he effaced the records of hers as far as possible, erasing her name and even casing her great obelisks at Karnak with brickwork.

[1] Br. II, pp. 121–2.

CHAPTER VIII

THUTMOSE III : WARS

THUTMOSE III, " THE KING WHO WROUGHT WITH
HIS SWORD "

INTERESTING as the reign of Queen Hatshepsut is, it was not a reign which added to the
strength or influence of Egypt. Little had been
done since the death of Thutmose I to assert the
national power. Thus when Thutmose III succeeded to the sole rule he was faced by just such a
general revolt of the subject peoples as has always
followed in the East upon any lack of vigour in the
governing body, as our own history in India has
often shown. Consequently the history of this
part of his reign is almost purely military ; at
least seventeen expeditions were made into Asia
during the forty-two years of his rule ; his military
and naval forces were more perfectly organized
than those of any earlier Pharaoh and the firm
hold he secured on his conquests led even the great
neighbour states of the Hittites, Babylon, and
rising Assyria to send him gifts. The king himself
took an active part in the war, being his own

THUTMOSE III

general and strategist, and leading his forces in person in the first campaign. This was directed against the revolting peoples of Palestine and Syria, and culminated in the siege of Megiddo, their city of refuge, which stands on a northern spur of the range of mountains running south-eastwards from Mount Carmel. The campaign is summarized thus :[1]

." The king himself, he led the way of his army, mighty at its head, like a flame of fire, the king who wrought with his sword. He went forth, none like him, slaying the barbarians, smiting Retenu, bringing their princes as living captives, their chariots wrought with gold, bound to their horses. The countries of Tehenu do obeisance because of the fame of His Majesty, with their tribute upon their backs. . . ."

Details are then given of the fighting in Palestine :

" Now it happened . . . the people, who were there in the city of Sharuhen, behold from Yeraza (in northern Judea) to the marshes of the earth (Upper Euphrates valley), had begun to revolt against His Majesty. [His Majesty] ordered a consultation with his valiant troops, saying as follows :[2] ' That [wretched] enemy, [the chief] of Kadesh has come and entered into Megiddo ; he [is there] at this moment. He has gathered to himself the chiefs of [all] the countries [which are] on the waters of Egypt (i.e. dependent lands)

[1] Br. II, p. 178, ll. 13-18.   [2] Br. II, p. 178.

and as far as Naharin (the Euphrates valley), consisting of the Kharu, the Kode, their horses, their troops. . . .' "

This confederation evidently represents the rallying of the Hyksos. Kadesh had apparently been the heart of their empire, and to the north-east of it had grown up the strong State of Mitanni, on the upper Euphrates valley. Beyond Mitanni the new State of Assyria was beginning to emerge on the east, while north-west, in Asia Minor, lay the powerful Kheti, the Hittites.

The wars of Ahmose, Amenhotep, and Thutmose I had expelled the Hyksos, driven them through Palestine and reduced the scattered groups of them both in Syria and Palestine to subjection, but since the early years of Thutmose, Egypt had failed to hold these lands, except southern Palestine, where Thutmose II's demonstration had instilled fear Mitanni and Kadesh seem now to have combined to rouse the whole of the north and even a few of the southern tribes in a final effort to thrust back dreaded Egypt. They occupied Megiddo as their gathering point, for it stood on a commanding hill above the Plain of Esdraelon, blocking the only northern route between the two ranges of the Lebanon. Behind this bulwark they seem to have gathered their entire force of allies and of treasure for the war, and could they hold it they would be secure in all their northern States. The freedom of their economic as well as political life depended upon keeping this pass against the Southern Empire,

for it was through the valley of the Orontes, which
it guarded, that all the trade and treasure of the
East passed into traffic with the Mediterranean
coasts. Phœnicia was thus vitally concerned, for
her life flourished on this sea-borne trade, and
already Tyre and Sidon had their outposts in " the
isles of the sea," trafficking with the cities of Cyprus
and Crete, the Mycenean towns of southern Greece
and the Ægean, and possibly already reaching out
along the coasts of southern Italy and Sicily to
touch the site of Carthage. Their trade with Egypt
too was frequent in times of peace, and probably
the Hyksos occupation had greatly developed this
for the time. It is this question of the ebb and
flow of commerce which lies at the root of most of
the political movements among the early states,
as in modern days.

The history of the campaign in Palestine goes
on to tell how on the march the Egyptians came to
the dangerous pass of Megiddo and the officers
voted for making a circuit as they feared to fall into
an ambush, but the king overruled them : " [Then
his majesty] commanded the entire army [to march
—upon] that road which threatened to be [narrow].
. . . He went forth at the head of his army himself showing [the way] by his own footsteps horse
behind [horse]." The army emerged safely from
the gully, and presently encountered the revolted
tribes. " [The enemy] went forth . . . in numerous battle array. . . ." Then the king at the head
of his troops seems to have led the charge, shouting

his war-cry and shattering the resistance, which cannot have been great at this point : " His majesty cried out to them. . . . They fell."[1] The Egyptians were not yet clear of the difficult country, and were still in danger of losing touch with one another. The rear was in Aruna (south of the Carmel ridge), while the van was debouching on the northern plain. The king took up a central position until the rear had joined up again, thus itself escaping from the risk of separation, and at the same time bringing double weight to bear on the enemy. Thutmose seems to have understood that secret of military success—concentration at the moment of attack. The record runs :[2] " Now the rear of the victorious army of his majesty was at the city of Aruna, the front was going forth to the valley (of Esdraelon). . . . Then [they] said in the presence of his majesty . . . ' Let the rear of this army come forth to us behind ; then shall they [also] fight against these barbarians ; then we shall not take thought for the rear of our army.' His majesty halted outside (on the north of the Pass), and waited there, protecting the rear of his victorious army." Thus the Egyptian forces made their way through the hostile country, sweeping through the valleys until all resistance was hemmed in at Megiddo, to which place Pharaoh now drew near. " Behold . . . when his majesty arrived at the south of Megiddo on the bank of the brook of Kina (a tributary of Kishon), the seventh

[1] Br. II, p. 182, ll. 10, 13.   [2] Br. II, p. 183, ll. 2-4.

hour was turning, by the sun (i.e. it was about
1 p.m.). Then was set up the camp of his majesty
and command was given to the whole army saying,
" Equip yourselves ! Prepare your weapons ! for
we shall advance to fight with that wretched foe
in the morning ! [Therefore] the king rested in
the royal tent, the [affairs] of the chiefs were
arranged, and the provisions of the attendants."[1]
This is a necessary halt for the staff to plan the
attack while the commissariat overhauls the main
body and sees to its well-being. " The watch of
the army went about, saying ' Steady of heart !
Steady of heart ! Watchful ! Watch for life at
the tent of the king.' One came to say to his
majesty, ' The land is well, and the infantry of the
South and North likewise.' " This appears to be a
despatch from Egypt to report on the smooth
working of civil and military affairs at home, so
that the king could go forward to the crucial
struggle at Megiddo with an easy mind. It suggests
too that the campaign was following a prearranged
course, and that Thutmose had planned to be at
this point at a given date, and thus reflects the
highly organized and methodical policy he carried
out. To meet this there was a confederacy of
northern States and of southern barbarians already
swept out of their own regions, and we get a very
different sense, in reading Thutmose's life, of the
relations of the tribes to Egypt from that familiar
to us in the Bible. The Chosen People are here

[1] Br. II, p. 183, ll. 16–24.

merely a group of tribes among the barbarians ; and Egypt, about to become the great dominant power is as much their master in 1500 B.C. as Rome was to be in A.D.

The siege of Megiddo at once took place, on May 15th :[1] " Year 23, first (month) of the 3rd season on the 21st day, the day of the feast of the new moon [corresponding to] the royal coronation, early in the morning, behold, command was given to the entire army to move. . . . His majesty went forth in a chariot of electrum, arrayed in his weapons of war, like Horus, the Smiter, lord of power, like Montu of Thebes, while his father, Amon, strengthened his arms. The southern wing of this army of his majesty was on a hill south of the Kina, the northern wing was at the north-west of Megiddo, while his majesty prevailed against them (the confederates) at the head of his army . . . they fled headlong to Megiddo in fear, abandoning their horses and their chariots of gold and silver. The people hauled them [up] pulling [them] by their clothing, into this city ; the people of this city having closed it against them [and lowered] clothing to pull them up into this city. Now if only the army of his majesty had not given their heart to plundering the things of the enemy, they would have captured Megiddo at this moment, when the wretched foe of Kadesh and the wretched foe of this city were hauled up in haste to bring them into this city. . . . Then were captured their horses,

[1] Br. II, p. 184, ll. 2–21.

their chariots of gold and silver were made spoil, their champions lay stretched out like fishes on the ground. The victorious army of his majesty went around counting their portions. . . . Then spake his majesty saying,[1] ' Had ye captured [this city] afterward, behold I would have given [thanks to] Re this day, because every chief of every country that had revolted is within it ; and because it is the capture of a thousand cities, this capture of Megiddo. Capture ye mightily, mightily.'

" [His majesty commanded] the officers of the troops to go . . . assigning to each his place. They measured this city, [surrounding it] with an enclosure, walled about with green timber of all their pleasant trees. His majesty himself was upon the fortifications east of this city, [inspect]ing. . . . It was walled about with a thick wall. . . . People were stationed to watch over the tent of his majesty, to whom it was said, ' Steady of heart ! Watch.' His majesty commanded saying, ' Let not one among them [come forth] outside, beyond this wall, except to come out in order to knock at the door of their fortification '[1] (i.e. to make submission.)

" Now all that his majesty did to this city, to that wretched foe and his wretched army, was recorded on each day by its (i.e. the day's) name. . . . Then it was recorded upon a roll of leather in the Temple of Amon this day."

This is the earliest detailed account of a cam-

[1] Br. II, p. 185, ll. 9-25   [1] Br. II, p. 186, ll. 1-18.
8

paign in history. It is evident that Thutmose, when he camped on the bank of the Kina, with Megiddo in sight on the hillside, had thrown out a force to the north-west of the town, hoping to cut it off from the western road to the sea, but had not quite done so. The main force of the enemy seems to have been awaiting the Egyptians on the south, and too far east of the town, reckoning on their rounding the ridge of Carmel by the right instead of forcing the pass. This error was fatal to the confederacy : had they held their Thermopylæ they might have inflicted a disaster on Egypt.

But the Egyptians in their turn made the mistake of flying on the spoil, and the wrath of Pharaoh wakes a keen response in the reader at the pity of it, that when one forward rush would have given him " a thousand cities," the ringleaders of the whole confederacy at one blow, he should thus have missed the capture. But the army, even of Egypt, had much to learn of discipline, and there had been little chance in late years for the training of such valiant officers as the two Ahmoses had been.

As a result of the fall of Megiddo the tribes gave in their submission :[1]

" Behold the chiefs of this country came to render their portions, to do obeisance to the fame of his majesty, to crave breath for their nostrils, because of the greatness of his power . . . bearing their gifts, consisting of silver, gold, lapis lazuli, malachite ; bringing clean grain, wine, large cattle and

[1] Br. II, p. 186, ll. 1-18.

small cattle. Each of the Kode . . . among them bore the tribute southward. Behold his majesty appointed the chiefs anew for [——] . . ."

The spoils taken at Megiddo are an interesting indication of the stage of civilization reached by these peoples, and show it to have been not unlike that of Mycenæ in Homeric times ; such items occur as :[1] " a chariot, wrought with gold, its pole of gold . . . a beautiful suit of bronze armour . . 7 poles of wood wrought with silver, belonging to the tent of that foe. . . ." ; and in the plunder taken a little later from the men of the Lebanon were " flat dishes of costly stone and gold . . . gold in rings found in the hands of the artificers, and silver in many rings. . . . A silver statue in beaten work—the head of gold, the staff with human faces ; six chairs of that foe, of ivory, ebony, and carob wood, wrought with gold, a statue of that foe, of ebony, wrought with gold, the head [of which] was inlaid with lapis-lazuli."[2] Ring-money of silver is in conspicuous use here as currency. This great success broke the spear-head of the confederacy, but many campaigns were to follow before the Empire of Egypt was assured. In them, as in the first, Thutmose III proves his grasp of the essentials of strategy.

The key to the northern area had been Megiddo, but to penetrate to its heart it was needful to get astride the great trade-route from west to east, and the easiest approach to this was by sea. Thus

[1] Br. II, p. 187, ll. 2-14.   [2] Br. II, p. 188, ll. 6, 11.

the king first scoured the Lebanon and planted a
fort there, then established new governors through
northern Palestine, taking their sons as hostages
to be educated in Egypt, and on his next campaigns
he continued this work. At last in his twenty-
ninth regnal year, his fifth campaign, he was ready
for the critical new move. His two main objectives
were first the seaports of Phœnicia and then the
strongholds of its up-country : Zahi, Tunip, and
finally the great Hyksos citadel, Kadesh.

The campaign opens, therefore, with a naval
operation, the fleet carrying the troops to the
siege of a great seaport whose fall was followed by
the reduction of Arvad and had possibly been
preceded by Tyre coming to terms. The booty
was immense in this fertile region, fruit and wine,
heaped and flowing, and grain countless as sand,
reaped from the sunny, terraced fields of the hill-
sides ; the army revelled, soaking itself with oil
and wine.

Thutmose meanwhile was receiving the submission of the rulers of all the small States along the
seaboard and its little river valleys, and the season
closed with his return in triumph by sea to Thebes.
It was in the sixth campaign that he reached his
second objective. Kadesh lay some thirty miles
inland on the Orontes, in a little plain between the
ranges of the Lebanon. The river and its small
western tributary, further connected perhaps by
a canal, formed a natural water-defence about
the city, within which was another moat, man-

made, and then a ring of high walls. This fortress
was thus worthy to have been the citadel of a great
empire, such as the Hyksos seem to have swayed,
and in it the last fragments of that race were now
besieged by Thutmose. The only account is short :[1]
" (His majesty) arrived at the city of Kadesh, overthrew it, cut down its groves, harvested its grain."
But these few words enable Professor Breasted to
reconstruct the scene and to show that the siege
lasted many months, since Thutmose had landed
his forces at Simyra after the spring rains and the
march was an easy one up the valley of the Eleu-
theros. He apparently used the same method of
siege as at Megiddo, building an enclosing wall of
the local timber and starving the enemy into
surrender. But while the city still held out against
his assaults it had encouraged fresh resistance in
lately conquered Arvad, a rising which Thutmose
punished drastically so soon as his hands were free
at Kadesh. As after his victory at Megiddo, he
found it necessary to drive the lesson home, and
spent two more years in doing so, organizing the
north as he had done the south, with new governors,
whose sons he educated at Thebes as before.
Meanwhile he had in mind a final advance eastwards, and for this he made ready by causing each
port and town to collect every sort of supplies,
so that the Phœnician region became a vast base
of operations ; " Loaves, oil, incense, wine, and
fruit " were brought in later ; from inland came

[1] Br. II, p. 198.

" much clean grain in the kernel, barley, incense, wine, and fruit."

The Hyksos were broken at Kadesh ; it now remained to deal with their chief allies the Mitanni, whose support had enabled the small towns like Tunip and Zahi in the plain between Orontes and Euphrates to stir up resistance and revolt in the coast towns, and who lay themselves about the Upper Euphrates and in the full stream of the traffic of East and West.

In his eighth campaign Thutmose came by sea to the port of Simyra, and followed his former route to Kadesh, thence he turned northwards down the Orontes valley and reduced such outposts of the enemy power as Katna and Sensar. He was now nearing Tunip, but we have no record of its capture. The enemy seem to have withdrawn before him to a place appointed on a southern spur of the Amanus range called " The Height of Wan," where a decisive victory set Thutmose free to make for the Euphrates, since troops from Aleppo which had barred the road seem to have been captured in the battle. The Naharin watershed was now completely at the disposal of Egypt, and Thutmose was soon at Carchemish on the Euphrates, the river which seemed to the Egyptians when they reached it a century earlier under Thutmose I " to follow upstream in flowing downstream," since its course was the opposite of the Nile's.

From the records of this campaign we read :[1]

[1] Br. II, p. 202, ll. 20-4.

" Behold his majesty was in the land of Retenu."
" Behold his majesty went forth capturing the towns
and laying waste the settlements of that [foe]
the king of Mitanni of wretched Naharin—he
pursued after them an *iter* of sailing ; not one looked
behind him, but fled, forsooth, like a herd of mountain goats ; yea, the horses fled. . . ." This
evidently describes Thutmose's penetration of the
Naharina, now by river and now overland, till he
reached the Euphrates and overthrew Carchemish,
and his officers hunted the rout across the river.
The king himself presently crossed it and set up a
boundary tablet to mark the first grip of Egypt
on this eastern bank, and another beside that of
Thutmose I on the western. Garnering the harvests of the vanquished as he went, he then followed
the stream down to the city of Niy, which he also
took.

" He set up a tablet east of this water ; he set
up another beside the tablet of his father." On
the southward march " His majesty arrived at the
city of Niy, going southward, when his majesty
returned, having set up his tablet in Naharin,
extending the boundaries of Egypt."

The officer Amenemhab who was with Thutmose
throughout these wars gives us another detailed
picture from this scene :[1] " Again another excellent
deed which the Lord of the Two Lands did in Niy.
He hunted 120 elephants for the sake of their
tusks and [——] I engaged the largest which was

[1] Br. II, p. 233, l. 9.

among them, which fought against his majesty ;
I cut off his hand (i.e. trunk) while he was alive
[before] his majesty, while I stood in the water
between two rocks."

This is a strange story. We should not have
expected to find elephants on the Euphrates, but
it is evident from this account that wild herds of
them roamed there as they now do in India. This
officer seems to have come to the rescue of Pharaoh
when the leader of the herd threatened him, and
having called off the huge beasts' attack to have
sheltered himself between rocks where the ele-
phant could only thrust in his trunk after him.
Cutting this off, Amenemhab would then render
the poor creature half helpless, and he would be
easily dispatched by the other hunters. This
campaign in Naharin marks the highest rise in the
power of Thutmose III, and indeed in that of
Egypt for all time. By the impression it made
among surrounding nations Egypt was admitted as
a power of the first rank in Western Asia, and gifts
of friendship, which she called tribute, came in from
all sides.

From Shinar, around Chaldæa came " real lapis
lazuli, artificial lapis lazuli, lapis lazuli of Babylon ";[1]
" Kheta the Great " sent " 8 silver rings . . . of
white precious stone a great block."

Here Egypt comes into her first official contact
with Kheta, the Hittites, a great power having a
capital at Pteria, on the Halys River, and thence

[1] Br. II, p. 204, ll. 10–13.

dominating all Asia Minor and presently also
Northern Syria down to the Orontes Valley, which
was to bring them into conflict with Egypt under
Ramses II. The Hittite record chamber has been
found, packed with clay tablets but their hieroglyphic alphabet has not yet been deciphered.
They were an Aryan people of the same type as
the modern Armenian, and gave the prominent
aquiline nose to the Hebrews and Canaanites and
other of their neighbours. They worked the iron
found in the hills of Asia Minor in the thirteenth
century B.C., and were a link between the Euphrates
and the West, sometimes dominating Assur and
using the cuneiform as well as a hieroglyphic
script. The former has just begun to be deciphered. They carved rocks in the same way
as the Egyptians, which show their influence
all over Western Asia. Their empire lasted
till the rise of Lydia, when Crœsus became their
lord.

In the Mediterranean too the backwash of
Pharaoh's campaigns was felt, for his fleets were
passing continually across that " Green Sea," as
Egyptians called it. Crete was in his hands, for a
golden dish exists which Thutmose III gave to his
" governor of the islands in the midst of the sea."
Cyprus (i.e. Isy) sent gifts of a kind, which show the
Cypriots to have been producers of metal-work,
as the lately recovered history of the Minoan
empire also declares them. They sent in one year
" 108 blocks of pure copper ; 5 blocks of lead ;

1,200 [pigs] of lead ; lapis lazuli, ivory, 1 tusk ;
2 staves of — wood."

On Thutmose's return to Thebes with all his aims
thus accomplished there was great national rejoicing, the echoes of which reach us in the great
Hymn of Victory of Amon-Re, the dignity and
beauty of which deserve that it should be studied
as a whole, though only fragments can be given
here.[1]

HYMN OF VICTORY

" Utterance of Amon-Re, Lord of Thebes
   Thou comest to me, thou exultest, seeing my
        beauty,
   O my son, my avenger, Menkheperre (Thutmose
        III), living forever.
   I shine for love of thee,
   I have given to thee might and victory against
        all countries,
   I have set thy fame (even) the fear of thee in all
        lands. . . .
   I have put the roaring of thy majesty among
        the Nine Bows.
   The chief of all countries are gathered in thy
        grasp. . . .
   I have felled thine enemies beneath thy sandals ;
   Thou hast smitten the [borders] of rebels accord-
        ing as I commanded thee.

[1] Br. II, p. 263.

The earth in its length and breadth, Westerners
    and Easterners are subject to thee,
Thou tramplest all countries, thy heart glad . . .
    etc., etc

CHAPTER IX

THUTMOSE III : ADMINISTRATION

THUS far in his career Thutmose III had proved himself the greatest strategist and the greatest conqueror Egypt had produced. No one of the thousands who used the proud Egyptian signature " triumphant " after their names had such a right to it as he, and it is no wonder that the glamour of his victories and the memory of all the riches and honour pouring in to his Court from the ends of the earth wove legends and folklore about his name for the latter days.

But the later years of his reign, though they run on uneventfully, earn him a far higher place among the great governors of the earth than even his conquests. Even regarding these he shows his statesmanship in the highest degree. Although his campaigns in the North from the ninth to the seventeenth form a less detailed and less eventful series than the first eight, they prove that his readiness and thoroughness did not fail. A revolt occurred in the Naharina as early as two years after its conquest, although the year before Thutmose had been at Lebanon and punished

Map of the **EGYPTIAN EMPIRE**

KHATTI
(HITTITES)

LIMIT OF EMPIRE

Carchemish

NAHARINA

AMANUS MTS

Height of Wan

Aleppo

Euphrates

Erkatu

Tunip

Niy

Qarqar

Sensar

Hamath

CYPRUS

Arvad

AMOR

Eleutherus R.

Kadesh

Ullaza

Ribleh

Byblos

Beirut

Sidon

Litani R.

Damascus

Tyre

Yenoam

Megiddo

Dor

Aruna

Gezer

Jerusalem

AMMON

Ashdod

Yeraza

Askalon

Lachish

MOAB

KABIRI

El Arish

Sharuhen

Arad

EDOM

OR

Pelusium

SHASU

0   100   200   300 *Miles*

three rebellious towns, work which he had to repeat
in this thirteenth campaign.   In each of these years,
however, he was easily master, thanks to the regular
system of supplies he had planned on the coast
and to the high discipline he maintained in fleet
and armies. Libyan mercenaries had long been
used with the Egyptian militia levies, but a new
force had grown greatly in numbers in his reign,
formed of the sea-raiding mercenaries known as
Sherden, perhaps kin of the Sardinians—men who
lived like the Norman adventurers of the ninth to
eleventh centuries A.D. plundering by sea or selling
their arms to the highest bidder. Thutmose seems
to have had well-disciplined troops of these men on
his northern campaigns. The severity with which
he put down the rebellions in Syria and Naharina
after a great battle with the men of Aleppo and
their allies at a place called Araina, probably on
the lower Orontes, seems to have finally broken
their spirit of independence, except in the case of
Kadesh and Tunip, which made a last effort in the
seventeenth campaign. This led to the second
siege of Kadesh, and of that we have a glimpse
from the career of Amenemhab. Thutmose appears
to have called for volunteers for the final assault :[1]
" His majesty sent forth every valiant man of his
army, in order to pierce the wall for the first time,
which Kadesh had made.   I (Amenemhab) was the
one who pierced it, being the first of all the valiant :
no other before me did."

[1] Br. II, p. 234, l. 1.

" Behold his majesty was upon the coast-road, in order to overthrow the city of Erkatu and the cities of Kana. . . ."[1] This was the forty-second year of Thutmose's reign, and his thoroughness now had its reward. No more risings are recorded, and all the northern provinces now pour their rich tributes steadily into Thebes. Their government seems to have been left in the hands of native families, whose scions were trained in Egypt, and by the third generation proved loyal vassals. Over them as viceroy of the whole wide northern dominion was the king's general, Thutiy, who is also described as prince and priest, favourite and scribe, governor of countries, pouring the tribute of land and sea into the treasury.

The imperial rule of Egypt, like that of the Moguls in India and all other eastern suzerains, rested on the collection of dues, usually in kind, and so the viceroys were in the first place finance ministers, tax-collectors. The tribute of these taxes went straight to the king's chests, and Thutmose was shrewd and masterful enough to set inspectors in the provinces to serve the double purpose of saving the poor from oppression and seeing that the wealth did not stick to the fingers of the under tax-gatherers. In all these matters similiar conditions imposed upon Thutmose and Charlemagne, with his " Missi dominici," similar methods.

The strong hand of the ruler was felt in the

[1] Br. II, p. 215, ll. 5, 6.

choice of reliable ministers, who swung his rod over the remotest delinquent.

The glory of gold and grain, of ivory and cedar, oils, Syrian dyes, wine and woven vestures set in a steady stream up the open mouths of the Nile. Cunning craftsmen and artists, sturdy labourers, horses and cattle trooped through the streets of Thebes ; some men manacled and led like beasts followed by wife and children into slavery ; others no doubt seeking to settle among " the fleshpots of Egypt." Probably famine followed Thutmose's sword in the rebellious districts, and the story of Jacob's sons driven to carry gifts down into Egypt to buy food for their little ones can only be one out of hundreds of such dramas. Many new types found homes in Egypt as serfs or craftsmen, and, mingling their blood with the Egyptians, began to change the racial type and also the character of the people to some appreciable extent.

Such a rush of prosperity was bound to relax the old, severe simplicity of the Egyptian, and this becomes visible. The dress was no longer a short kilt but an elaborate quilted robe, and the wigs were as long and curled as ours in the age of Anne.

The ritual of the temples became more and more elaborate as their wealth increased, and Amon's ascendancy was growing by leaps and bounds. The Hymn of Victory shows an inextricable bond between king and god : each is the other's defender, and the balance between their powers as perfect, the supremacy as hard to assign as between Papacy and Empire at a later day. Thutmose was indeed a faithful son of the Church of his day, and his grant of three cities of Lebanon, with lands in Egypt to Amon as a perpetual property, is as important politically as Pepin's grant of the Exarchate to St. Peter. It was the beginning of a land-dominion in each case which almost compelled the holders to assume a temporal power ruinous in the end to their spiritual claims. But the struggle between Church and State was not yet. Thutmose ruled supreme, and his subjects said, like the Romans, " It is a god that hath given us this Peace." For the first time in the world's life one mind swayed the lives of men from Ararat to the Soudan. The Hymn makes no idle boasts when it makes Amon say :

" I have come causing thee to smite the Asiatics, . . .
   I have come causing thee to smite the eastern
      land . . .
   I have come causing thee to smite the western
      land.
   Keftyew and Cyprus are in terror.
   The lands of Mitanni tremble under fear of thee . .
   Lord of fear in the water, unapproachable.
   Those who are in the midst of the Great Green
      hear thy roarings.
   The isles of the Utentyew [belong] to the might
      of thy prowess.
   Thou hast smitten the Sand-dwellers as living
      captives."[1]

[1] Br. II, p. 264.

Like Rome, Egypt flung open the doors between
these peoples, and for the first time they shared
a common traffic. Thebes became the mart of the
world, controlling equally the gold of Nubia and
riches of the East. For the first time this general
exchange made silver cheaper than gold, which
has held its place as the standard ever since ; and
the silver-ring money of Syria and the isles yielded
to the weight of gold sent regularly now for twenty
years from Nubia by Pharaoh's treasurer-viceroy.
This man, Nehi, seems to have kept Kush quietly
progressive all the time his master was engaged
in Syria. On his return from the great eighth
campaign on the Euphrates Thutmose found his
halls at Thebes thronged with the spoils of Punt.
Wine was coming in too from the oases of the
western desert, now held for Pharaoh by his
nomarch of Thinis, Intef. Nubia enjoyed peace
until near the end of the reign, when raiders had
to be punished, and in the fiftieth year one such
punitive force once more cleared out the canal at
the first cataract. One hundred and eight Nubian
towns are recorded in the list of his captives, and
his frontier reached to the fourth cataract ; but this
does not seem to have involved any real advance or
much more than border warfare.

The twelve comparatively peaceful years that
followed his empire-building campaigns enabled
Pharaoh to show that he was second to none of his
great ancestors in love and skill for architecture.
From Karnak to Kush, in his own and his sons'

9

reigns, the windings of the Nile were beautified
by the most magnificent temples, in which statuary,
columned halls, brilliant paintings, and the adorn-
ments of bronze, ivory, and gold vied with one
another, and set standards of art not soon reached
and not in every case surpassed even by the Greeks.
Karnak held his father's hall in the State-temple,
but this had been disordered by Hatshepsut, and
her obelisks made his attempts to restore it at
first incomplete. His finest work had been as yet
his own mortuary temple to Amon in the western
plain ; but in his twenty-fourth year Thutmose III
began to build great halls of colonnades on the east
end of his father's temple ; the largest was 140 feet
long and stood for six centuries bearing his name
" Menkeperre is Glorious in Monuments." Here
too, he had fashioned portrait statues of all his
ancestors, some of which still exist. Far away in
Kush he had at least six temples raised or restored
and others are found in the towns of Phœnicia
while his garrisons in Naharina may well have had
their temples too. A feature of building in this
period was the obelisk, and of these Thutmose built
many, though he had defaced those of Hatshepsut
with brick casings. Six of his stood at Karnak
and at Heliopolis. Not one remains in Egypt, but
in Rome is the " Lateran " obelisk, with his inscription on its southern face,[1] " Thutmose III he made
it as his monument for his father Amon-Re, Lord
of Thebes, erecting for him a single obelisk in the

[1] Br. II, p. 252.

forecourt of the temple over against Karnak, as
the first beginning of erecting a single obelisk in
Thebes, that he might be given life."

The " Cleopatra's Needle " we have on the
Thames-side is really one of a pair he built in
Heliopolis. The Romans first took it down the
Nile to a temple of the Cæsars in Alexandria in 13 or
12 B.C. It was brought to London in 1878. It stands
68½ feet high. Its fellow crossed the Mediterranean
and Atlantic to New York two years later.

Perhaps the most significant aspect of Thutmose's
rule is that related in the records of Rekhmire, his
vizier. These records give a picture of the vizier's
daily work, and show the wonderfully high standard
demanded by the king in the conduct of his courts
of justice, and the orderly system and etiquette
by which it was carried out. There is no hint of
servility, and yet the personal control and influence
of Thutmose is evident as the main motive in the
work. We are told first of Thutmose's instructions
to Rekhmire when he appoints him to the Hall of
the Vizier :[1] " Be watchful over all that is done
therein. Behold, it is a support of the whole land."
Then the king goes on to say that the petitioners
shall come from the south and the north and the
whole land, and urges Rekhmire not to delegate
the work to any subordinate. " Mayest thou see
to it thyself . . . to do everything according to the
right thereof. It is an abomination of the god to
show partiality . . . thou shalt regard him who

[1] Br. II, pp. 268, 269.

is known to thee like him who is unknown to thee, and him who is near to, like him who is far." He bids him not " to avoid a petitioner, nor nod thy head when he speaks," and not to punish a man without making clear to him his offence. The sound conception of true majesty appears in this injunction :

" Be not enraged toward a man unjustly . . . show forth the fear of thee . . . a prince is a prince of whom one is afraid. So, the true dread of a prince is to do justice." But he adds a caution against the familiarity that breeds contempt : " Be not known to the people ; and they shall not say : ' He is (only) a man ! ' "

The scene of the audience is clearly drawn :[1] ". . . while hearing in the Hall of the Vizier, he shall sit upon a (special) chair, with a rug upon the floor, and a daïs upon it, a cushion under his back, a cushion under his feet, and a baton in his hand, the 40 skins (of records) shall be open before him.

" Then the magnates of the South (Rekhmire's own province) shall stand in the two aisles before him, while the master of the privy chamber is on his right, the receiver of income on his left, the scribes of the Vizier at his either hand ; one corresponding to another, with each man at his proper place. One shall be heard after another, without allowing one who is behind to be heard before one who is in front."

Furthermore : " . . . He shall go in to Pharaoh

[1] Br. II, p. 273, ll. 7–15.

before the Chief Treasurer ; he shall wait at the
northern flagstaff. Then the vizier shall come
proceeding from the gate of the great double façade
(i.e. the Palace of State of the Two Lands). . . .
Then the Chief Treasurer he shall come to meet
him and shall report to him, saying ' All thy affairs
are sound and prosperous, etc.' . . . Then the
Vizier, he shall report to the Chief Treasurer,
saying ' All thy affairs are sound and prosperous,
etc.'

" Now after each has reported to the other, of
the two officials, then the Vizier shall send to open
every gate of the king's house, to cause to go in
all that goes in, and to cause to go out all that
goes out likewise, by his messenger, who shall
cause it to be put in writing.

" . . . His messenger shall seize the mayors
and village sheiks for the judgement hall . . . it is
he (Rekhmire) who brings in the officials of the
districts : it is he who sends them out ; they
report to him the affairs of their districts.

" Every property list is brought to him ; it is
he who seals it.

" It is he who administers the (gift) lands in all
regions. One shall put every petition in writing,
not permitting that he petition orally. . . .

" It is he who gathers the troops, moving in
attendance upon the king, in journeying northward or southward. . . . It is he who despatches
to cut down trees according to the decision in
the king's house.

" It is he who despatches the official staff to attend to the water-supply in the whole land.

" It is he who despatches the mayors and village sheiks to plough for harvest-time."

These records are from Rekhmire's tomb, which is also decorated with scenes of all his work, inspecting all manner of crafts, civil and naval offices, receiving and weighing tribute, etc, etc.

These are invaluable documents to show the complete organization of the Egyptian State.

In the first place, the " 40 skins " indicate that there existed a recognized body of laws or cases whereby the judge's decision could be given. These would of course be old laws, having no doubt a sanctity similar to Edward the Confessor's code in our own history.

The relationship of the Vizier and the Chief Treasurer is extremely interesting, showing unmistakably that they were each a check upon the other, precisely like the Nawab and the Dewan in a native Indian State. Thus the Vizier, the executive officer, was responsible to the Treasurer for all funds expended, such as judicial costs, wages of troops, or of building operations, while the Treasurer, on the other hand, only received the dues by means of the Vizier's messengers, who " seize the mayors and village sheiks " when these are backward in paying their collections. There is a vivid picture of the mayors being hailed into the treasury office in the decorations of the tomb of one of the lords of Beni-hassan. They are ranged in a queue kneeling, while slaves or minor officers haul each forward in turn. This makes the reader realize the difference between a modern court, where moral or social force of law suffices, and an ancient court, even of the best kind, where actual force was still needed. Under the Egyptian Vizier " it is clear that many distinct State departments existed." Perhaps the most important was the irrigation office, for in Egypt the Nile movements and the mathematical calculations based upon them made it essential that one will should control the water-supplies of the whole Two Lands ; and it followed from this that the orders for " ploughing for the harvest " must also come from the central authority, and not, as in Saxon England, be left to a village meeting to decide.

The Vizier claims control even of the military and naval levies, as well as the going in and coming out of traffic, i.e. the import and export trade ; he is thus an incarnate Whitehall, a whole Cabinet rolled into one, but of course acting through delegates or " messengers " for each department.

CHAPTER X

AMENHOTEP II

EGYPT'S greatest Pharaoh, Thutmose III, slept with his fathers when his reign had lasted over half a century, and his son Amenhotep II reigned in his stead.

Physically, as a leader in war and as a builder of magnificent monuments, he was worthy of his great father. Over six feet in height and strong in proportion, he had a bow which none but he could bend, and this was buried with him in the valley of the tombs of the kings, where he still rests. He had acted as regent with his father for only a year when the old king's death let loose a storm of revolt in all the north lands. Promptly and effectually Amenhotep led the avenging armies and furnished an example of bravery. At Shemesh-Edom on the Orontes "himself fought hand to hand." "His majesty crossed over the ford of the Orontes. . . . His majesty raised his arm, in order to see the end of the earth ; his majesty descried a few Asiatics coming on horses (——) coming at a gallop (the sign " *rkrk* " conveys the beat of hoofs). . . . They retreated when his

majesty looked at one of them. Then his majesty
overthrew their chief with his spear. . . . Behold
he carried away this Asiatic—his horses, his chariot,
and all his weapons of battle."[1] The tall, kingly
figure is plain to see, shading his eyes to pierce the
desert glare, casting his spear beyond the range of
other men. So he made his way out to the
Naharina, and the city of Niy received him, the
new generations bred up under his father's rule,
" men and women were upon their walls, praising
his majesty." His return was a triumphal march,
leading captive seven unhappy princes, hundreds
of nobles and their wives, with a booty of gold and
gold vessels weighing 1,657½ lbs. troy and nearly
100,000 lbs. of copper. His vengeance was bar-
baric : " When his majesty returned with joy of
heart to see his father, Amon, he slew with his own
weapon the seven princes, who had been in the
district of Tikhsi, and had been placed head downward at the prow of his majesty's barge, the name
of which was ' Okheprure-is-the-establisher-of-the-
Two-Lands.'[2] One (i.e. Pharaoh) hanged the six
men of those fallen ones, before the wall of Thebes,
those hands (of the other slain) likewise. Then the
other fallen one was taken up river to Nubia and
hanged on the wall of Napata (the southern frontier
town) in order to cause to be manifest the victories
of his majesty." This end was served, and Nubia
remained quiet, the exhibition of frightfulness
inspiring due terror, and most of the reign was free

[1] Br. II, p. 307, l. 17.　　[2] Br. II, p. 313, ll. 1-7.

for works of grandeur. The first work needed was to clear out the access to the great quarries which even Thutmose III had not done : [His majesty found] the quarry chambers which are in Troja (near Memphis) beginning to go to ruin since the times that were before '' (the Hyksos period).

This marked the beginning of the greatest building period of the empire. Amenhotep II completed his father's unfinished temples in Kush, and repaired some of the disorder wrought by Hatshepsut in the Karnak temple, built a small mortuary temple there, and others at Memphis and Heliopolis, which have not remained. His reign lasted a quarter of a century. He seems to have been at peace almost all that time, and it is surprising that so little is known of him.

The son who succeeded him, Thutmose IV, had a shorter reign, which opened like his father's with revolt in the North. This he quickly suppressed by a march to Naharin, and returned triumphant, bearing with him cedars of Lebanon to build the State barge of Amon, and long trains of captives from southern Palestine to till his own temple lands. Such incidents show that the captivity of Israel in Babylon was no exceptional disaster.

The reasons for such a policy were probably threefold—first to root out resistance in the subject State ; secondly, as the Old Testament shows, to secure cheap labour or re-people devastated areas ; and thirdly, perhaps to infuse new vigour

MODELS SHOWING BAKING, BREWING AND SACRIFICE

into a native population either exhausted or decadent.

On the reliefs of the period the wretched captives are to be seen dragged in halters like cattle ; and indeed there seems to have been small distinction in their masters' minds between the troops of beasts and human captives whom they led. A similar punitive expedition to Nubia in this king's eighth year was equally effective, and Thebes received once more boatloads of spoil and gangs of captive negroes.

But Thutmose IV perhaps recognized that force alone could not hold the subject provinces ; from some motive he chose to ally himself with the Mitanni of northern Syria by marriage. On No. 24 of the Tel-el-Amarna letters at Berlin it is written that his offer was made seven times, like the seven years that Jacob wrought for Rachel, but the marriage finally took place and the queen, Mutemua, may have brought new ideas and customs with her into the Egyptian Court. Her son was the famous Memnon or Amenhotep III, no less warlike than his father and grandfather, but noted especially among the Greeks for his love of hunting. The regular story is repeated in his reign of the rising of " the foe, Kush, the wretched," and of the subsequent carnage : " the chiefs were overthrown in their valleys, cast down in their blood, one upon another."[1] A second revolt was suppressed by his general, Mermose : " Ibhet had been haughty,

[1] Br. II, p. 336, ll. 9-11.

great things were in their hearts," and it was the Pharaohs only who might with impunity harbour " great things in their hearts." Throughout this latter part of the Middle Empire the tone of the Court and people, as well as the Pharaoh, echoes the note of the conqueror. Power, wealth, fame, the constant sight of triumphs, and the parade of captives had their effect on the mind of the nation, and a pride grew there like that of Spain, mistress of the New World ; it seems to have undermined the best qualities of the Egyptians in a similar way, and to have found its most acute development, as in Spain, among the ranks of the highly privileged and largely parasitic priesthood.

Amon, or Amon-Re, had been the leading god since Thebes had thrown off the Hyksos rule, and the Theban god Montu, sometimes identified as an aspect of Re, is, so to speak, the patron god of the conquering Pharaohs, who are said to shine in battle " like the might of Montu." It was at the altar of the god Amon that the sacrificial slaughter of each triumph took place, the Pharaoh, as son of the god, himself cutting down the victims. Such religious rites not merely permitted but encouraged in priest and people alike a pride and cruelty which could not but provoke reaction in their own nature as well as among the conquered. Ishtar, or Ashtaroth, Baal, Sebek the crocodile, and other gods thus became names of terror and symbols of horrid sufferings and their priests accursed in the eyes of all reformers.

At this time the queens assume a more prominent place beside the Pharaohs, and Memnon's queen is especially notable, though her racial origin has not been clearly discovered. Her name was Ti, or Tiy, and in the following passage the notice of her parents by name and the grandeur of her husband combine to show that the queen's position was to be deliberately raised :[1] " Live . . . King Amenhotep, who is given life, and the Great King's wife Tiy, who liveth. The name of her father is Yuya, the name of her mother is Thuya. She is the wife of a mighty king whose southern boundary is as far as Karoy, northern as far as Naharin."

While his wife Thuya, or Tuaa, was an Egyptian, Yuaa, or Aay, as Yuya is also called, may have been a foreigner, very possibly one of the Syrian princes brought to live in the Egyptian Court as hostages for the good behaviour of their people. If so, Tiy, although born and brought up in Egypt, had foreign blood in her veins. Her father was a priest of Min, the Egyptian equivalent of Pan, or Adonis, and perhaps not in sympathy with the corrupt priesthood of Amon-Re. He stood in favour with Thutmose IV and his Mitannian queen, Mutemua, and was made a prince in his latter days. The marriage of Tiy to Memnon took place while they both were very young—ten and twelve respectively ; and we have one glimpse into their life in these words :[2] " His Majesty commanded to make a lake for the Great King's wife Tiy, in her city of

[1] Br. II, p. 345, ll. 4–8.   [2] Br. II, p. 349, ll. 4–8.

Zerukha. Its length is 3,700 cubits; its width 700 cubits. His Majesty celebrated the feast of the opening of the lake in the 3rd month of the 1st season, day 16, when His Majesty sailed thereon in the royal barge ' Aton-gleams.' " The influence of Queen Tiy seems to have been very great throughout her life, and possibly accounts for the unusual character of her son's reign. Of her husband, Memnon, we are told in the usual fanciful language of the Court writers: " The Good God, Golden, shining in the chariot, like the rising of the sun; great in strength, strong in might, mighty-hearted like him who dwells in Thebes [Montu]; smiting Naharin with his sword."[1] "Marvel which happened to His Majesty. One came to say to His Majesty, ' There are wild cattle upon these highlands, as far as the region of [Sheta].' His Majesty sailed downstream in the royal barge, Khammat, at the time of evening, beginning the goodly way, and arriving in safety at the region of [Sheta] at the time of morning. His Majesty appeared (in a chariot) his whole army·being behind him. The commanders and the citizens of all the army in its entirety and the children with them were commanded to keep watch over the wild cattle. Behold His Majesty commanded to cause that these wild cattle be surrounded by a wall with an enclosure. His Majesty commanded to count all these wild cattle.

" Statement of [that which] His Majesty [captured] in the hunt on this day : 56 wild cattle.

[1] Br. II, p. 346, ll. 1–14; p. 347, ll. 3, 4.

" Statement of lions which His Majesty brought down with his own arrows from year 1 to year 10 :—fierce lions, 102."

Memnon's greatest title to fame is perhaps in the realm of architecture. It was now that all the new tendencies came to their full beauty. The quarries which Amenhotep II had reopened were now yielding ample materials ; the wealth of the empire conquered by Thutmose III was flowing steadily into Thebes, and therewith a stream of able craftsmen to work the precious metals and co-operate with native Egyptian artists, bringing the art motives of Crete and Babylon to blend with those of the Nile valley.

The use of the column seemingly originated in Egypt and was carried to perfection in this reign. It seems to have been a reproduction in stone of the ordinary wooden post upholding the roof-beam in an Egyptian house. This in its earliest form was merely a palm-trunk, sunk into the earth for a foot or more and clamped in its place by a hard-beaten mound of clay. Between the top of the trunk-shaft and the cross-beam it was usual to put a block of wood to take the stress of the weight. In this and the clay foot-mound we have perhaps the origin of capital and base used with the column in all but Doric work. From such early beginnings the Egyptians worked out beautiful pillars, usually shaped in imitation of some natural form. At first merely supports to roofing, they came to be used in greater numbers, until their value in long ranks upholding the roof of a portico or temple led to the perfection of the idea in the colonnaded hall of the temple at Karnak. Egypt was thus undoubtedly the school in which the Greeks learned the value of this architectural form.

Another form, developed at the same time, has never been used in such perfection elsewhere. This was the avenue or double line of monuments of a like shape marking the approach to a great palace or temple. Amenhotep III not only completed the temple at Karnak, but he made it one with Luxor by turning the mile and a half between them into a great garden and lining the roadway with a double rank of great stone sphinxes. The riverside, too, was given a stately wharf and ascent to the temples.

That Egypt retained that sea-power which Thutmose III had exercised in the Levant and neighbouring waters is evidenced by the record of Amenhotep, son of Hapi, Memnon's officer, which also shows the regular numbering of the people and the replacing of retired men by recruits. It runs :[1] " I levied the classes of my lord, my pen reckoned the numbers of millions, I put them in [classes] in the place of their [elders] : the staff of old age as his beloved son.

" I taxed the houses with the numbers belonging thereto, I divided the (gangs) and their houses, I filled out the subjects (i.e. Egyptians) with the best of the captivity. . . . I placed troops at the

[1] Br. II, p. 374, ll. 17–28.

heads of the ways to turn back the foreigners in their places. The two regions were surrounded with a watch, scouting for the Sand-rangers. I did likewise at the heads of the river-mouths (i.e. Delta mouths), which were closed under my troops except to the troops of (sea-warriors). I was the guide of their ways, they depended on my command."

CHAPTER XI

IKHNATON (1358 B.C.)

THE tendencies which seem to have been developing since Thutmose's conquests, on the one hand, towards a rigid form of organization controlled in the main by the priesthood of Amon, and on the other hand the growing influence of the various foreigners who had entered the land, culminated in the next reign in a temporary revolution accomplished by the king himself, who taught a monotheistic creed and overthrew the priestly domination, with the artificial conventions it enforced both in life and art.

The life of Amenhotep IV, who called himself Aakh-uen-aton, or Ikhnaton, is full of fascinating problems, and repays close study. He was the son of Tiy, famous as Memnon's queen. He had possibly inherited a foreign strain, and this may in part account for his original genius. He was always subject to illness, being epileptic, yet he reigned twenty years and imposed his ideas upon the whole land.

Queen Tiy had been the power beside the throne during the last ten years of Memnon's reign, and

the changes that followed no doubt had her support.
Iknaton taught that the supreme god was Aton,
with whom he identified the disk of the sun ; his
own name meant " the spirit-soul of Aton," and he
raised altars to " the heat that is in Aton." We
may thus read into his teaching the conception of
a Spirit, behind the life-giving principle of Light, a
single, creative Being, with whom men may have
contact through the enjoyment of His works,
especially light, heat, and the life of Nature which
they foster. The king seems to have been himself
a poet of a high order, if the hymns to Aton are
rightly called his. In one of these there exists an
almost exact forerunner of Psalm civ, as the following extracts show :[1]

" The world is in darkness like the dead.
  Every lion cometh forth from his den ; all
      serpents sting.
  Darkness reigns.
  When Thou risest in the horizon . . . the
      darkness is banished.
  . . . Then in all the world they do their work.
  All trees and plants flourish. . . .
  . . .The birds flutter in their marshes. . .
  All sheep dance upon their feet.
  How manifold are all Thy works !
  Thou didst create the earth according to Thy
      desire—men, all cattle . . . all that are
      upon the earth."

[1] Weigall, " Akhnaton," pp. 155-6.

The simplicity of the prayers to Aton is sharply contrasted with the style of the worship of Amon, as may be seen in the prayer of Merire I, high-priest of the One god, and ardent supporter of the reforms :[1] " Grant Thou thy beloved Son, living in truth, Lord of the Two Lands, (Ikhnaton) that he may live with thee forever, that the Great King's wife, his beloved Nefernefruaton-Nofretete, living forever and ever, may be by his side, doing that which pleases Thy heart, seeing all that Thou hast made, every day." They say of the king :[2] " Thy beloved son presents truth before thy beautiful face " ; and again : " whose heart is satisfied with truth, whose abomination is lying " ; while Iknaton himself uses these words : " It is my oath by the truth, that which my heart shall speak ; that which I do not speak is falsity ; forever and ever."

The career of Iknaton suggests a comparison with certain of the great mystic kings of the Indian States, especially Asoka and his pattern, Buddha. Nowhere in the West is " the philosopher on the throne " to be found carrying out so consistently, and to so disastrous an end from the world's point of view, the practice of a new, essentially mystical faith.

Iknaton devoted himself to teaching this new faith to the Court and people, and he lavished rewards upon the converts among his nobility. He identified his god with the ancient Egyptian deity " Ra-Harmarkis " and thus in a sense with

[1] Br. II, 406, l. 4.   [2] Br. II, p. 409, l. 23.

Re-Amon, but he was bitterly opposed to the Amon-worship of Thebes, which the priests had made the universal religion of Egypt. Consequently conflict was bound to follow the first few years of his teaching. The king made the break the more marked by changing his name from *Amon*-hotep to Aakhuen*aton*, and removing his Court from Thebes, the town of Amon, to a new site 160 miles above Cairo, where he built a beautiful city called the " Horizon of Aton "—Akhetaton, or Khutenaton.

Opposition must have been general and increasing, for such an advance from pantheism to monotheism cannot be effected lastingly except among a people, like the Arabs of Mahomet's day, who are in some respects prepared for it. As Prof. Breasted says, Iknaton was " a brave soul," disseminating " ideas far beyond and above the capacity of his age to understand." For the time being he prevailed. Art was reformed on the pattern of the early work of the archaic period and a true return to nature, discarding the conventions which limited artists to the use of special poses, etc. There is, consequently, a grace and freedom in the sculpture and friezes of this period equal to the best early Italians ; and he seems to have carried this return to simplicity into the Court life and the literature, appearing with his family at any function and using plain terms instead of the inflated pomposity of the regular ritual and Court language used hitherto. Thus the magnificence and grandeur of the empire was discarded deliberately in this reform of internal affairs, but at the same time it was coming to an end in the external realm of conquest and government.

Physically unfit and preoccupied as Iknaton was with the world of ideas, religion, and philosophy, he paid no heed to the upkeep of the material greatness of Egypt. Such neglect, added to the attacks upon their ancient beliefs, could not fail to stir the country to opposition. The personal hold which the king's charm and power exerted hardly sufficed to the close of his reign, and reading the pathetic appeals for help and reinforcements sent vainly by the soldiers who strove to hold outposts in Syria, we cannot wonder that the reforms to which the empire was sacrificed crashed to dust on his death.

A great conspiracy of Amorite and Syrian vassals, with the ever present Hittite raiders, set the whole of the newly acquired Asiatic provinces in a blaze of revolt ; but it was allowed to burn unchecked by this prince who " sought peace and ensued it."

Asiatics sought refuge in Egypt pleading,[1] " others have been placed in their abodes . . . their town laid waste . . . their countries are starving, they live like goats of the mountains. . . . A few of the Asiatics, who know not how they should live, have come [begg]ing [a home in the domain] of Pharaoh after the manner of your father's father since the beginning. . . ."

From the ruins of Akhetaton, which was aban-

[1] Br. III, p. 7, ll. 4-12.

doned and never inhabited after Ikhnaton's reign, a great historical treasure has been recovered, consisting of a long series of official papers—the correspondence of the Egyptian officers in Syria with the Court. They are known by the modern name of the place " Tel-el-Amarna."[1] These letters show a state of gradually growing confusion in Syria. The governors of the frontier and coast towns make valiant efforts to withstand the steady weight of the Hittite movement southwards ; but it was the overflow of a race and no mere military invasion. Had Egypt turned all her treasure and arms on to this one aim it is doubtful whether she could have warded off the northern power ; for her provincial officers to do so was to court disaster. Yet, like so many another in later history, these men staked their all on the belief that the Empire would never desert them. Year after year they sent urgent appeals.

Ramman-nirari of Nuhassi (probably Aleppo) was grandson of an officer of Thutmose III, and seems to have inherited his charge of the town. He reports " the king of Hatti," the Hittites, advancing against him, and continues : " And if my lord has decided to march out, then let my lord send one of his counsellors, together with his soldiers and his chariots. . . ." (Letter 37.)

Another officer, Abd-Asratu, writes more appealingly : " At the feet of my lord, the king, seven times and seven times, I fall. Verily I am a

[1] " Tel el Amarna Letters," Hugo Winckler.

servant of the king and a dog of his house, and the whole land of Amurri (probably Amor) I guard for the king, my lord. I have repeatedly said to Pahanati my (superior) plenipotentiary, that he should bring the guard for the defence of the king's land. . . . May my lord the king ask him if I do not defend Simyra and Ullaza." (Letter 38.)

This is followed by an appeal from the city of Tunip in which complaint is first made against Aziru, an officer who was betraying the interests of Egypt and acting with the Hittites, while pretending in his despatches that he was still loyal. The contrast between the great days of the Empire and these latter evil times is acute :

" My lord, Dunip, your servant, speaks, saying— Who formerly could have plundered Dunip, without being plundered by Manahbiria (i.e. Thutmose III). And now for twenty years we have been sending to the king, our lord, but our messengers remain with the king, our lord. And now Aziru, your servant . . . in the land of Hatat has captured them (probably dependents of Tunip) by force. If his (the king's) soldiers and chariots come too late, Aziru will make us like the city of Ni (i.e. desolate). . . .

" If however we have to mourn, the king of Egypt will mourn over those things which Aziru has done. . . . And when Aziru enters Simyra, Aziru will do to us as he pleases, in the territory of our lord the king, and on account of these things, our lord will have to lament. And now Dunip,

your city, weeps, and her tears are running, and
there is no help for us. For twenty years we have
been sending to our lord the king, the king of
Egypt, but there has not come to us a word from
our lord, not one." (Letter 41.)

The traitor Aziru presently writes to a friend at
Court to exculpate himself from the charges brought
against him : " Verily you (Dudu) are my father
and my lord, and I am your son, and the lands of
Amurri are your lands and my house is your house.
And whatever your desire is, write, and I will give
whatever is your wish.

" Behold you sit before my lord, the king . . .
slanders against me before our lord ? . . . do not
permit . . . do not allow. . . . And if the king
does not love me, but hates me, what shall I say
then ? " (Letter 44.)

Another document shows Pharaoh reproaching
Aziru and laying fresh commands upon him, despite
the suspicion under which he lies at court :

" To the prince of Amurra : the king, your lord.

" The prince of Gebal, your brother. . . . ' Take
me and bring me into my city. . . .' Thus he
speaks to you.

" Behold you write to the king, your lord : ' I
am your servant ' . . . and yet you have committed
a fault in taking a prince . . . from his city. . . .
And when he was living in Sidon, you delivered him
up to the princes . . . as if you did not know the
hatred of the people. . . . And even if you do
right, still all the words are not true with regard

to which you write . . . so the king will be obliged to think :—All that you say is not true.

" And verily a prince has heard, that you have made peace with the prince of Kades, food and drink mutually to deliver ; and it is true. . . . Whatever be your conduct between them, you are not upon the side of the king, your lord. . . ."

" Behold, your lord, the king, sends you the names of the enemies of the king in this letter, by the hand of Hanni, the king's messenger ; therefore send them to your lord, the king, and let not one of them escape. And chains of bronze should be placed on their feet. . . ." (Letter 50.)

It is not surprising that Ikhnaton's mild reproaches did nothing to allay the disloyalty of Aziru and his fellow-traitors. There is a series of letters from the loyal officer Rib-addi of Gebal to Ikhnaton and to patrons at his Court, describing the progress of the invaders, the loss of town after town, the flight of prominent persons to Tyre ; telling how Sidon and Simyra and Beirut are acting with the enemy, until at last even Gebal itself revolts and the one loyal voice is silenced. Nothing in history is more pathetic reading than the impassioned appeals of this honest soldier for the help that never comes. The note of hope changes through reproach to despair, and the final cry, " Send ships to bring me alive, with the gods," passes into the silence of captivity or death.

Rib-addi of Gebal to Pharaoh : " . . . Let the action of Abd-asirta, the cur, be clear to my lord, the king, that the lands of my lord, the king, are coming into his power, and the [king] will have to lament over his land. Behold now, Simyra is a court and house of my lord . . . and he encamps in . . . Furthermore, if . . . people come before . . . Gebal . . . capture Gebal . . . and is difficult . . . the lands of my lord. Further, let the king send his officer . . . in order that that cur may not carry off the property of your gods, and that he may not rejoice (?) if he seizes Gebal. For Gebal as well as Hikubta belongs to the king." (Letter 53.)

" To Haiapa. . . . Verily you are a sage. . . . Why do you delay telling the king to send troops to occupy Simyra ? For Abd-asirta is a cur, and the land of the king is going over to him, in order to save its life. For its subsistence is greatly endangered because of the Habiri. Also send 50 pairs (?) of horses, and 200 footmen ; then station yourselves at Sigata, in front of him, until the troops march out. In order that he may not bring together all the Habiri and capture Sigata and Ambi and . . . there is not one place." (Letter 54.)

" And moreover if the king should march forth, though all the lands were in rebellion against him what could they do to us ? In this case they would altogether do good, but I am very greatly afraid that there is no man to rescue me out of their hands ; like a bird which is caught in a net, so shall I be in Gebal. Why will you neglect your land ? Behold I wrote thus to the king's palace, but they paid no attention to my message. Verily Amanappa is with you ; ask him, he knows about it, and has seen the distress, which has come upon me. . . . Verily I am thus mindful day and night." (Letter 55.)

" Furthermore . . . now he has mustered all the Habiri against Sigata and Ambi, and they have taken . . . those two cities. And behold there is no place where I can go. . . . Further you are a great lord, O that you may not neglect this affair ! " (Letter 56.)

" Further, will you not come up to Amurri ? Day and night, they are waiting to see if troops will not be sent." (Letter 59.)

" If I should make an agreement with Abd-asista, as Japa-addi and Zimrida (did), I should be rescued. . . . If you do not command this (aid) I shall leave the city and flee . . . with the people who love me." (Letter 61.)

" . . . Behold, I remain shut up in my city, I am not strong enough to go out of its gate. (Letter 64.) Their sons, their daughters, and the timbers of their houses are no more, having been given to Jarimuta for their sustenance. Verily three times three years have passed over me, and for two years my grain has grown. (Now however in the third year) there is no grain for us to eat. Who should have sown it ? " (Letter 69.)

" Behold Tyre has acted rebelliously. . . . I have deposited my property in Tyre, in order that it might be at my disposition. Verily they (of

Tyre) killed their commander, and also my sister
and her sons. I had sent my sister's daughters to
Tyre from fear of Abdasirta." (Letter 70.)

" As long as I am in the city I guard it for my lord.
But . . . my brother has incited the city, so as
to deliver it to Abd-asirta's sons. O may not my
lord, the king, neglect the city! For there is a
very great deal of silver and gold in it; in its
temples there is much property if they capture
it! . . . Behold I have sent your servant, my son,
to my lord, the king, and may the king send him
immediately, with men for the occupation of the
city. . . ." (Letter 71.)

" . . . Why did my lord, the king, write to me,
saying ' Defend yourself, and then you will be
protected ' ? Wherewith shall I defend it against
my enemies ? . . . If the king does not protect
his servant." (Letter 74.)

". . . If I write bad news to my lrod, then someone
says, ' Why do you write bad news ? ' If my words
were regarded, then Aziru would be captured, as (I
said). Verily I am the king's knight." (Letter 75.)

" Furthermore, why does the king compare me
with the princes ? The princes—their towns belong
to them, their sheiks are subject to them ; but I—
my towns belong to Aziru. . . . What dogs the
sons of Abd-asirta are ! And they act according
to their hearts' wish, and cause the king's cities to
go up in smoke." (Letter 76.)

" Abd-asirta's sons have entered the land of
Amurri, and to them the whole land belongs.

(Only) Simyra and Irkata are left to the deputy
And behold in Simyra am I, for the deputy was
hard pressed, on account of the enemies and aban
doned Gebal . . . all the troops have run away
out of Simyra."   (Letter 78.)

"Let the king know that the king of Hatti takes
away all the Kutaim lands, the king of Mitani, the
king of Nahrim . . . the dog takes away."   (Letter 79.

"The ships and people of Simyra, Beirut and
Sidon, all of them that are in Amurru are pressing
me hard, and behold now Japa-addi and Aziru
have attacked me, and verily he has seized my
ship.   And behold they have thus sailed forth into
the ocean, in order to capture my ships . . . my
subjects are intending to desert—a messenger whom
I had sent . . . was not able to enter Simyra, fo
all the roads were cut off."   (Letter 81.)

"Behold Haib has delivered over Simyra; let
not the king overlook this deed, namely the killing
of the deputy."   (Letter 94.)

". . . The city has been in rebellion against
me; and verily, the city says 'A shameful deed
such as has not been committed from eternity, has
been committed against us.'"   (Letter 100.)

". . . And you, do not abandon (me); if there
are no troops there now, send ships to bring me
alive, with the gods to my lord."   (Letter 105.)

"This is a letter from the city of Irkata to our
lord the king.   Irkata and its elders fall down
We have bolted the gate until the breath of the
king comes to us. . . ."   (Letter 122.)

Ammumpira of Berut : " Furthermore as to the
man from Gebal, who is with me, I am indeed guard-
ing him until the king shall care for his servant.
Further let my lord the king know of the action
of his (Rib-addi's) brother, who is in Gebal—that
he has given the sons of Rib-addi who is with
me, to the adversaries of the king in Amurri."
(Letter 129.)

Akissi of Katna : " O my lord just as Damascus
in the land of Ubi stretches out her hand to your
feet, so also Katna stretches out her hand to your
feet. . . ." (Letter 139.)

Namiawaza, another apparently disloyal captain :
" Verily I and my soldiers and my chariots, together
with my brothers, and my Habiri and my Suti,
are at the disposition of the troops, whenever my
lord, the king, commands."

Itakkama : " O my lord, I am your servant,
and Namiawaza has made me evil in your eyes,
O my lord. And while making me evil in your
eyes, he has been occupying the whole territory
of my father in the land of Kades, and my towns,
he has given over to fire. . . . And behold Namiawaza has delivered all the cities of my lord, the king,
to the Habiri in the land of Kades and in Ubi."
(Letter 146.)

Finally, even Tyre is attacked, and on land the
invaders press up against Jerusalem. The prince,
Abi-milki of Tyre, writes : " Zimrida of Sidon,
and Aziru, rebel against the king, and the people
of Arwad have conferred with one another, and

have collected their ships, their chariots and their *niru* people (i.e. hired troops) in order to seize Tyre, handmaid of the king. . . . Tyre they were not able to conquer, but they have conquered Simyra. . . . Why does our lord, the king, turn away from the country ? '' (Letter 150.)

Abdhiba of Jerusalem speaks out plainly : " The king's whole land which has begun hostilities with me will be lost. Behold the territory of Siri as far as Ginti-Kirmil, its princes are wholly lost, and hostility prevails against me. . . . As long as ships were upon the sea, the strong arm of the king occupied Naharina and Kas, but now the Habiri are occupying the king's cities. There remains not one prince to my lord the king, every one is ruined. Behold Turbasa has been slain at the gate of Zilu, and the king remains inactive ! Behold Zimrida of Lachish—his servants are seeking to seize him in order to kill him. Japti-Addi has been slain at the gate of Zilu, and the king is inactive ! . . . ask him. Let the king take care of his land . . . (send) troops to the land of Jerusalem. For if no troops come in this year, the whole territory of my lord, the king, will be lost." (Letter 181.)

Thus the tide of Egyptian glory ebbed quickly back from the Syrian land, until not only Naharina, but the Orontes Valley, the coast, and even the highlands of Palestine threw off the yoke of Pharaoh, while Ikhnaton devoted his whole powers to the internal warfare against the religion of Amon and the sway of his priests. Complete as his success seemed in Egypt, it cost the Empire, and even so it could not last for it had not the weight of national feeling behind it, nor even the prop of a strong ruling house. In a few years Ikhnaton's work had vanished like " a dream that departed," but its effects on the Empire were never repaired, and the influence of later Pharaohs in Palestine and the Levant was never more than temporary. Even Ramses II, with all his campaigns, achieved no more than the checking of Hittite inroads. The Hittite power continued to sway the Syrian lands as far as Philistia, and Ramses' march to the Naharina was no more than a momentary raid.

CHAPTER XII

TUTENKHAMON (1350 B.C.)

WHEN Ikhnaton died he left no son, but several daughters, and the husbands of two of these in turn succeeded to the throne. The first, Sakere, reigned less than three years, and seems to have attempted to maintain Ikhnaton's ideas ; but the second, Tutenkhamon, returned to the old gods. He was only sixteen at his accession, and seems only to have reigned four years. His name was Tutenkhaton, and possibly he was in favour of the worship of Aton, for at Thebes he extended the temple of Aton ; but the religious reaction to Amon worship seems to have been too strong for him : he changed his name to Tutenkh-amon, and also restored buildings dedicated to that god at Thebes. He quitted the city of the Horizon of Aton and returned to Thebes, and Aton's cities quickly relapsed into ruins, so utterly deserted that it was not till 1888 that the famous Tell-el-Amarna letters, left in a brick chamber in the ruins of Akhetaton were re-discovered. They had lain there for over thirty centuries !

Such neglect speaks volumes for the triumph

of the old Amon worship, and it seems likely that
Tutenkhamon relied on the priesthood for support,
and that they had recovered mastery of the political
reins in Egypt. The names of Ikhnaton and his
god were erased everywhere. Short as it was, the
reign of Tutenkhamon seems to have been a success ;
his control of Nubia was evidently complete, and it
is possible that he recovered some influence in
Palestine. His viceroy in Nubia was Huy, who
ruled from El Kab to Napata, so that this province
was as large as in the days of Memnon. It is from
the tomb inscriptions of this officer Huy that our
knowledge of this reign comes.

Tutenkhamon is there shown sumptuously en-
throned to receive the tribute of Kush at the hands
of the viceroy. It includes gold and myrrh, ivory,
apes, and peacocks ; and the viceroy's boat is
shown, most elaborately carved and gilded. A
brother of Huy, named Amenhotep, is also shown
bringing tribute, and is entitled " Viceroy of the
North." It is doubtful whether this is more than
an attempt to show Tutenkhamon to be as great a
ruler as his predecessors. On the other hand, the
claim may have a real basis. Amenhotep presents
" the produce of Retenu, the wretched," " silver,
gold, lapis lazuli, malachite, every splendid, costly
stone " ; and this is just such tribute as Palestine
had formerly yielded. There is evidence too that
Huy had served in Palestine under a victorious
king, who could hardly be other than Tutenkhamon.
Further scenes show Asiastics received by the royal

officer with such phrases as,[1] " The chiefs of [all countries] that knew not Egypt since the time of the god (i.e. since Ikhnaton's reforms began) are craving peace from His Majesty," " The chiefs of Retenu the Upper are craving peace," " There shall be no revolters in thy time." In these scenes the king is represented on his throne, surrounded by piles of the precious metals, rich furniture, and chariots, and the truth of this presentation has been astonishingly confirmed in our own days by the discovery of his tomb in 1922.

The romance of this discovery rivals that of the fables of our childhood. Perhaps, indeed, the marvellous caves full of gold and jewels that we read of in the stories of Sindbad and Aladdin and " The Arabian Nights " are based on some dim memory in men's minds of the sealed tombs of the Pharaohs, full of treasures so carefully hidden away that the knowledge of the way to them was lost. In 1922 explorers had been already working for many years in the Valley of the Royal Tombs at Thebes, seeking the burial-places of such Pharaohs as had not already been discovered, most of them already plundered. France, Germany, Britain, and America had all had some share in the work ; but it was to an English nobleman that the prize fell in November, 1922. From his own lips London heard the story of how " for eight empty years " Lord Carnarvon and Mr. Howard Carter poured out time, labour, and money on a fruitless search.

[1] Br. II, p. 424, l. 8, 12.

STRING AND BEAD DOLLS

In one small area, near the tomb of Ramses VI, their workmen removed no less than 70,000 tons of rubble without result. But when the new season opened in autumn Mr. Carter was again at work, and only three days had passed when he came upon the first of a flight of steps, obviously leading down to some tomb. Would it be that of an official or a king ? Hopes rose high when the seal of the royal necropolis was deciphered, and some thought it might be the burial-place of Thutmose II ; but the tombs had been so systematically plundered that it might still prove to be empty. When all the steps had been uncovered the excavators found the entrance blocked by a wall, sealed with the royal seal ; but this had been so hurriedly covered in that the sealings were blurred. At last one was made out with the cartouche of Tutenkhamon. It was, then, a king's tomb ; but the wall had clearly been pierced and then closed up again, so it was most probable that thieves had visited it. When the entrance was made it was found to lead into a passage twenty-seven feet long, closed by a second wall, which also had been broken through and reclosed. By the time the workmen had cleared this approach Lord Carnarvon had arrived from England, and he and his companion in toil could together solve the great secret of the centuries. Lord Carnarvon has told with what scrupulous care a hole was opened in the wall, bit by bit, until it was large enough to admit a man's head. " We must have a look," he said, and then let the actual finder go forward first. With a lighted candle in his hand Mr. Carter looked in, and for two or three minutes Lord Carnarvon waited in breathless silence. At last he asked, " Can you see anything ? " And Carter's reply, " Yes, yes ; it is wonderful," assured him of treasure trove. An experienced Egyptologist who saw the sight shortly afterwards described it as " A most extraordinary sight—beyond anything I had ever conceived possible." They looked into a room about twelve feet by twenty-four feet in size, piled full of the most costly and beautiful things—couches, beds, alabaster vases, tables, and seats exquisitely inlaid ; parts of a chariot, statues of the king, chests and boxes which were found to be full of jewels and fine linen. Practically everything was of the most elaborate design and richest execution, surpassing even the finest art of our own civilization, and together bearing a staggering witness to the glory and wealth of the Pharaohs of Ancient Egypt.

This treasure chamber was the antechamber to the tomb of King Tutenkhamon, and for weeks the world followed intently the progress of the excavators. The extreme difficulty of their task became gradually apparent, for the rare fabrics were ready to turn to dust at a touch. British and American researchers pooled all their skill and experience to secure the unique relics from destruction. The delicate garments and fine linen had to be photographed layer by layer in the chests to catch the design of the ornament, and then lifted out with extreme care. Lord Carnarvon related that one of his first orders was for a mile and a half of wadding ! One garment was decorated with no less than 300 beads and rosettes ; others were of the finest woven tapestry, unmatched in the modern world. Two of the king's war-coats were wrought, the one of gold, glass, and semi-precious stones, the other of a network of porcelain pendants tied and clasped with gold. On one of his staves the figures of an Asiatic and a Nubian, intertwined, witnessed to his dominion of the North and South, while pictures of his conquered foes were inlaid on his throne and chariot.

It was not until the antechamber had been patiently emptied piece by piece of these treasures that the explorers could advance to the actual tomb chamber, and it was then too late in the season to continue the work. The inner chamber was explored, the king's sarcophagus found intact, and the season's work ended with the closing and sealing of the tomb, great iron doors having been made in readiness. The burial chamber was similar in size to the other, and to each there was a smaller room attached. The actual tomb was almost filled by the wooden shrine, covered with gold, inlaid with blue faience, and containing a whole series of inner shrines. At the east end of the chamber a second gorgeous shrine was surmounted by figures of four goddesses as graceful and lifelike as the best Greek work. No historical records

were found to throw light on the critical events
of this transitional reign, nor is it likely that any
but ritual texts would be placed in the tomb.
Evidences of haste in the stacking of the treasures
and the closing of the approach seem to suggest
that the young Pharaoh died suddenly, leaving
no one to succeed to them. The sudden death of
Lord Carnarvon only a few weeks after the work
ended adds a note of modern tragedy to this strange
story.

Whatever remains to be discovered concerning
Tutenkhamon, it seems clear that it was in his
day that Egypt returned from monotheism to the
worship of her ancient gods, with the priests of
Amon supreme.

This restoration was emphasized and consolidated
by the career of Harmhab, a general in the employ-
ment of Ikhnaton, who had fought in his wars
and those of Tutenkhamon, passed with ability and
favour through the period of reform, and under
the restoration came to pre-eminence through the
support of the Theban priesthood. From the
governorship of his own district he rose to be the
" chief mouth," or viceroy of all Egypt. Finally
he was called to the throne by the priests, and
married a sister-in-law of Ikhnaton, and the
restoration was now complete : " Behold all the
land was in joy, they cried out to heaven ; great
and small they took up the jubilation ; the whole
land was rejoicing. After the completion of this
(coronation) feast in Luxor, Amon, King of Gods,

returned in peace to Thebes." "He (Harmhab)
restored the temples (from) the pools in the (Delta)
marshes to Nubia. . . . Re rejoiced when he saw
them which had been found ruined aforetime. He
(Harmhab) raised up their temples."

But Harmhab's real claim to remembrance is
as a great administrator and just judge, relieving
oppression and bringing the extortionate lower
officials to trial. The inscriptions tell of a long
series of inquisitions which he, like our Henry II,
made into the condition of the poor and their
treatment by those in power :[1] " Behold, His
Majesty spent the whole time seeking the welfare
of Egypt and searching out instances [of oppression]
in the land."

His enactments are precise : " If there be a poor
man who pays the dues of the breweries and kitchens
of the Pharaoh to the two deputies [and he be robbed
of his goods and his craft, my majesty commands :
that every officer who seizeth the dues] and taketh
the craft of any citizen of the army or of any
person who is in the whole land, the law shall be
executed against him, in that his nose shall be cut
off, and he shall be sent to Tharu (Rhino-colura)."

[2]" When the officers of the Pharaoh's house of
offerings have gone about tax-collecting in the towns,
to take [katha-plant] [they have seized the slaves
of the people and kept them at work] for 6 or 7
days. . . . It shall be done likewise against them."

---

[1] Br. III, p. 25, l. 18 ; p. 26, ll. 8-14.
[2] Br. III, p. 27, ll. 11-14.

" The two divisions of troops which are in the field, one in the southern region, the other in the northern region, stole hides in the whole land, not passing a year, without applying the [brand] of [the royal house to cattle which were not due to them, thereby increasing] their number and stealing that which was stamped from them. They went out from house to house, beating and [plundering] without leaving a hide for the people. . . . A wretched case is this, therefore it shall be done likewise."

[1] " I have improved this entire land. . . . I have sailed it. . . . I have learned its whole interior, I have travelled it entirely in its midst. . ."

[2] " Now as for any official or any priest (of whom it) shall be heard saying, ' He sits to execute judgement . . . and he commits a crime against justice therein ; it shall be against him a capital crime."

[1] Br, III, p. 31, l. 5 *et seq*.
[2] Br. III, p. 32, ll. 1-4.

CHAPTER XIII

RAMSES I AND II

WITH this reign Egypt passes under the rule of a new Dynasty (XIX), better known than others because its kings left such plentiful memorials of themselves, but not really so powerful or important as those from the twelfth to the eighteenth. The first Pharaoh is Ramses I, but little is known of him beyond his name and that his son and successor, the more famous Seti I, ruled jointly with him for a year. Seti was one of the great warrior kings of Egypt, and the attempt to re-establish over the western countries of Asia the empire of Egypt which Ikhnaton had allowed to collapse was the main interest of this dynasty. The old temple order in Egypt was restored and firm, the old ideals of conquest and bloodshed prevailed again, and the desire for glory led these Pharaohs to extravagant lengths. They blazoned their own great deeds on the monuments, and built great tombs and temples ; but, not content with this, some, like Ramses II, replaced with their own name the names of earlier builders, and so tried to take to themselves the credit of greater works than their own. Their warfare was directed mainly against the great Hittite power ; but despite the display of activity and the parade of captives and sacrifices they made its results seem to have been on the whole negative. Ramses II brought the Hittites to consent to a treaty, but the gradual pressure of the nations converging upon Egypt from north and east and west was not really stemmed, much less driven back, and the history of the dynasties henceforth is a long, slow story of defeat, lasting, indeed, another thousand years, but showing less and less independence, and from 950 B.C. they were scarcely Egyptian at all : Libyans, Nubians, Saites succeeding one another on the throne, until finally the independence of Egypt disappears under Persia, Macedon, and Rome.

With the reign of Seti I began a series of vigorous wars to reaffirm the power of Egypt in Syria :[1] " One came to say to his Majesty, ' The vanquished Shasu (Bedwin, including Hebrew nomads) they plan rebellion. Their tribal chiefs are gathered together, rising against the Asiatics of Kharu (Hor). They have taken to cursing and quarrelling, each of them slaying his neighbour and they disregard the laws of the palace.'"

The heart of his Majesty was glad on account of it : " Lo, as for the Good God, he rejoices to begin battle, he is delighted to enter into it, his heart is satisfied at seeing blood, he cuts off the

[1] Br. III, p. 52, ll. 1-12.

heads of the rebellious-hearted. He loves an hour
of battle, more than a day of rejoicing. His
Majesty slays them at one time. He leaves not a
limb among them, and he that escapes his hand,
as a living captive is carried off to Egypt : " Some
were there sacrificed by Seti himself. Marching
from a base at Tchar (near Al-Arish) Seti beat the
nomads and passed through Palestine to Syria,
receiving tribute everywhere and securing the
coast-line as in the days of Thutmose III. He did
not encounter the Hittites in force till the third
campaign, when a great battle was fought against
them. The Egyptian recorders glorify Seti for his
exploits, but no practical result is evident from this
battle. Seti is thus described :[1] " Mighty Bull,
ready-horned, mighty-hearted, smiting the Asiatics,
beating down the Hittites, slaying their chiefs,
overthrown in their blood, charging among them
like a tongue of fire, making them as that which is
not. . . . He has smitten the land of Kheta,
causing the cowardly rebels to cease."

Much of this adulation is no doubt exaggerated
and due to the delight of the priests of Amon in
the devout worshipper of their god ; it is comparable
perhaps to the praises lavished upon Norman kings
by monkish chroniclers. Still Seti was undoubtedly
a fine man and a great king ; it is impossible to
consider portraits of him without recognizing in
them a nobility of line, strikingly akin to the
noblest and most refined modern heads.

[1] Br. III, p. 72, ll. 20-23.

Seti spent the latter part of his reign in collecting and using materials for the further glory of Amon. He had the erasures made by Ikhnaton replaced by new carving; he led expeditions into the southern desert to try to restore old routes to the gold-mines near the Red Sea, and to dig new wells and he had the quarries fully worked. The need for new wells is vividly described :[1] " How evil is the way without water ! It is as with a traveller whose mouth is parched. How shall their throat be cooled, how shall he quench their thirst, for the lowland is far away, and the highland is vast The thirsty man cries out for himself against a fatal country. . . . Make haste ! Let me take counsel of their needs. I will make for them a supply for preserving them alive so that they will thank God in my name, in after years. . . ."

An interesting detail tells of the supplies furnished to the native troops or gangs, 1,000 of whom were sent to the quarries at Silsileh :[2] " His Majesty increased that which was furnished to the army in ointment, ox-flesh, and plentiful vegetables without limit. Every man among them had 20 deben (i.e. 4 lb.) of bread daily, [2] bundles of vegetables a roast of flesh ; and 2 linen garments monthly They worked with a loving heart for His Majesty. . . ."

Among his many buildings the most famous and noteworthy is the great temple at Abydos, made of white limestone and called by the Greeks the

[1] Br. III, p. 82, ll. 2.   [2] Br. III, p. 90, ll. 15-19.

" Memnonium." It is on the corridor wall here that the list of Egyptian kings is carved from Menes onwards, without which the history of Egypt could not have been understood. Seven gods were to be worshipped in this temple—Horus, Isis, Osiris, Amon, Harmakhis, Ptah, and Seti I ; and such a list is very significant. It shows how important were still the antique gods Horus, Harmakhis, and Ptah of Memphis, though Amon of Thebes ranked as supreme. The worship of Isis and Osiris too was fully grown, and the Pharaoh himself, long recognized as the son of the god, now takes his place among them as altogether divine. Egypt and Rome alike allowed their sovereigns homage as gods while yet living out their mortal lives on earth, but the Pharaohs were essentially gods of war, whereas Vergil salutes his emperor with the famous line : " It is a god who hath given us this peace." There is nothing in Egyptian history comparable to the Pax Romana of the Empire, unless it be the close of the reign of Thutmose III.

RAMSES II (1292 B.C.)

If it could be said of Seti, " His heart is satisfied at seeing blood," still more was it true of Ramses II that he rejoiced in war as a means to renown. He took up the long-drawn struggle with the Hittites in the fourth year of his reign, and for seventeen years led the campaigns in Palestine and Syria.

The contest was a drawn one, and ended in a treaty which recognized the equal might of the two powers. This was the end of Ramses' wars, but there was no end of the record of them and of the king's personal prowess : they form the main theme of many of the scenes on the great monuments of his reign, which lasted sixty-seven years, and " was one of the greatest calamities that fell upon Egypt," as Dr. Budge maintains ; for Egypt was no longer gaining either in extent or in the use of her resources. She was indeed losing in virility and character—the wealth and ease procured in earlier reigns leading her people to relax their thrift and industry, while they employed the captives and borrowed the ideas of the peoples around them. The parallel with sixteenth century Spain or fifteenth century Venice becomes ever closer—the easily acquired riches and power in each case undermining the main strength of the native race when it becomes imperial, and this is in each case accompanied by a hardening of the tissues of government, till a rigid, lifeless autocracy is formed which forbids the criticism or opposition by which fresh life might be infused.

The reign, disastrous in its effects, is full of historical material and interest. The record of the wars gives the world the first detailed account of a campaign in which the plan and the objective are clearly shown, with their strategical reasons and the tactical adaptations of them to meet the sudden emergency ; the treaty is also happily preserved

RAMSES II

in full, and provides one of the few clues to the understanding of the position of the Hittites.

The important campaign is the first, in which occurred the closely fought struggle at Kadesh. The Hittite king Muthenra was at the head of a larger body of Hittite and confederate troops than had previously been seen; for they had not merely invaded but settled all North Syria and the Naharina during the reigns of Ikhnaton and his successors. On the other hand, Ramses, who had been subduing troubles in Nubia and Libya, had an immense force, consisting only in part of Egyptian soldiery, but largely of vassal and mercenary auxiliaries— always a sign of the decline of any military power. Four divisions marched behind him through Palestine, and as he pressed on to Kadesh, the southern stronghold of the confederate enemy, Pharaoh outpaced his generals. Misled by two decoys whom he captured he rashly encamped on the north-west of the town with only one division, that of " Amon," leaving the next, that of Re, to ford a stream and join him; the two other division were several miles to the south and widely strung out. But Muthenra, whom the decoys declared to have retired northwards, was in hiding with his entire force just behind the city. As Pharaoh moved north-west, Muthenra stole east and south under cover of the town, and fell upon the " Re " division just as it had crossed a tributary of the Orontes in loose marching order. Pharaoh meanwhile had captured two more Hittite scouts,

12

and by torture had learned from them the truth. Hastily calling his staff, while the men of " Amon " were encamping, he sent aides to call in the belated southern divisions, but was interrupted by panic in the half-pitched camp, unto which refugees from the smitten second division (Re) were now pouring, stampeding it itself. The moment was vital : Ramses seized it, called on his Egyptian guards to follow, and flung himself on the Hittite chariotry as they drove the men of Re before them There were 2,500 chariots, each manned by a Hittite warrior and two confederates, and these were rapidly surrounding the Pharaoh. He perceives one chance : the enemy pressing west after the fugitives leave the eastern wing thin ; on this weak spot he flings his tiny force of picked troops, with such fury that they drive it in and hunt some of the attackers back into the river. In doing so they leave the camp open, and fortunately for Ramses the Hittite charioteers fall upon the spoil and so give him a breathing space. The men of Amon and Re, perhaps, rally, an unexpected force of recruits appears, and the chariots are beaten off. All this time Muthenra remains with his infantry in reserve east of the river ; what follows is not clear, beyond the fact that both parties hold their ground until the division of Ptah, hastily summoned by the Vizier, struggles in at sunset, on which the Hittites retire into the city, and Pharaoh is able to draw off his troops in safety and return presently to Egypt. The belated division of Sutekh

seems to have retired independently, probably to
the base camp on the coast.

For this campaign there are fortunately two
authorities : the Poem of Pentaur, the work of
some poet laureate of the day, and the comparatively curt and vivid official military report.
The first describes the Hittite chariotry as [1] " an
exceeding great multitude, without its like. They
covered the mountains and the valleys ; they move
like grasshoppers with their multitude " ; " an
exceedingly numerous multitude, like the sand,
being three people to each span (i.e. chariot). Now
they had made their combinations : among every
three youths was one man of the vanquished of
Kheta (i.e. the victorious Hittites), equipped with
all the weapons of battle. . . ." " They came
forth from the southern side of Kadesh, and they
cut through the division of Re in its middle, while
they were marching without knowing, and without
being drawn up for battle. The infantry and
chariotry of His Majesty retreated before them."
" He was like Baal in his hour." " The great span
which bore His Majesty, called : ' Victory in
Thebes ' from the great stables of Ramses (II), was
in the midst of the leaders (? staff). His Majesty
halted in the rout (of flying troops) ; then he
charged into the foe, the vanquished (!) of Kheta,
being alone by himself and none other with him.
When His Majesty went to look behind him, he

[1] Br. III, p. 138, ll. 13-15 ; p. 140, 4-13 ; p. 140, l. 16-
p. 141, ll. 1-5.

found 2,500 chariotry surrounding him, in his way out . . . being 3 men to a span, acting in unison."

The official account describes the enemy's ruse :[1] " There came two Shasu to speak to His Majesty as follows : . . .' the vanquished chief of Kheta sits in the land of Aleppo on the north of Tunip. He fears because of Pharaoh, Light, Perfection, Health, to come southward. Now these Shasu spake these words . . . falsely, the vanquished chief of Kheta made them come to spy where His Majesty was, in order to cause the army of His Majesty not to draw up for fighting him. . . ."

" Then, as His Majesty sat upon a throne of gold, there arrived a scout (Egyptian) . . . and he brought two scouts of the vanquished chief of Kheta. . . . His Majesty said to them : ' What are ye ? ' They said : ' As for us, the vanquished chief of the Kheta has caused that we should come to spy out where His Majesty is.' Said His Majesty to them, ' Ha ! Where is he ? the vanquished chief of Kheta ? Behold I have heard saying : " He is in the land of Aleppo." ' Said they, ' See the vanquished chief of Kheta is stationed, together with many countries which he has brought with him by force, being every country which is in the districts of the land of Kheta, the land of Naharin, and all Kode (i.e. all of Asia Minor not included in Kheta), . . . See they are standing drawn up for battle, behind Kadesh the Deceitful.' "

" Then the Vizier was ordered to hasten the army

[1] Br. III, pp. 144-6.

of His Majesty, while they were marching on the south of Shabtuna (i.e. Ribleh), in order to bring them to the place where His Majesty was (8 miles north). Lo, while His Majesty sat talking with the princes, the vanquished chief of Kheta came, and the numerous countries which were with him. They crossed over the channel on the south of Kadesh and charged into the army of His Majesty while they were marching, and not expecting it. . . ."

[1]" His Majesty hurled them headlong, one upon another, into the Orontes. ' I charged all countries while I was alone, my infantry and my chariotry having forsaken me. Not one among them stood to turn about. . . .' "

It is clear from both accounts that Pharaoh's conduct of the march was somewhat over confident and careless, as might be expected from the Egyptian attitude of superiority. Yet their chief arm the chariotry, was one borrowed from these very Asiatic lands. Horses were not known in Egypt, to judge by the inscriptions, till the Hyksos invasions.

This makes the chariot duel between them at Kadesh, and its pictured history, the more interesting. The statement that Ramses ' charged all countries ' alone is wild exaggeration ; he had at least his bodyguard—no doubt the prime core of the division ; yet there was enough basis of truth in it to furnish Egypt with pride in his valour, and he seems to have taken unending joy in it, and had the story reproduced in picture form, as well as in

[1] Br. III, p. 147, l. 14.

poem and prose, so often that six versions still remain in Upper Egyptian temples and add much detail to the account—the Vizier, for instance, being seen starting himself for reinforcements, besides sending a despatch rider. This indecisive battle consequently bulks much more largely in Egyptian history than its immediate effect warrants; yet it is full of very real significance as a key to the character and tendencies of this transitional reign, leading to Egypt's decadence. The boastful, scornful temper of king and people cries out in every line ; to see the pictures alone would lead one to imagine the battle a smashing victory, and Ramses the greatest of conquerors ; in fact, the vice of false patriotism, belittling the neighbour nations to glorify one's own—a vice of which almost all historians are guilty in one form or another—is nowhere more blatant and unashamed than here. The downfall is obviously imminent of such a nation as this.

A very different set of impressions is produced by reading the terms of the treaty to which eight more years of varying conflicts brought the rival powers to agree. Nothing seems to have been achieved but the usual waste and weariness on both sides : no boundary line can be marked out between them ; neither can claim allegiance of the other ; it is a mere statement of equality and cessation of war.

The sequel to the battle of Kadesh had been revolt on the part of Palestine as well as Syria and the Naharina. Ramses subdued them, recapturing

Askalon and the country we know as Philistia,
some twenty-four cities of Western Galilee, the
Haaran region east of the upper Jordan, as well
as the district of Tabor, the most southern to which
the Hittites ever descended. His conquest of
Naharina can have been little more than a raid,
for the Hittite influence was all-powerful so far
north. Ramses II claims, like Thutmose, to
receive tribute from Assur, Shinar, and Cyprus,
but this can mean at most only the receipt of
formal courtesies ; the Hittite power he never
seriously damaged, as the treaty and evidence of
peaceful intercourse between the countries later
in his reign go to prove. A full copy of the treaty
remains in Egyptian, on the wall of the hypostyle
at Karnak, and part of the end of it on the Rames-
seum ; they are translations made from a probably
Babylonian original, and are in a long-winded
style, full of the minutely careful repetitions that
belong to such legal documents in all ages. The
main points are :

(i) Cessation of war between Kheta and Egypt.
(ii) A defensive alliance.
(iii) A mutual return of political refugees and of
emigrants.
(iv.) The seal of the gods.

The arrival of the commissioners is thus
described :[1] " There came the (Egyptian) king's
messenger, the deputy and butler . . . [bringing

[1] Br. III, p. 166, ll. 1-5.

to the king] Ramses II the messenger of [Kheta, Ter]-teseb and the [second messenger] of Kheta [bearing a silver tablet] which the great chief of the Kheta, Khetasar [caused], to be brought to Pharaoh, to crave peace. . . . "

This King Khetasar had just succeeded on the death of Muthenra, and very possibly Egypt had sent a proposal for peace as a courtesy on this occasion, although the Hittites are here represented as " craving " for peace from Pharaoh ; there is no direct evidence, for the Egyptian phrases of the following passage must not be taken at their face-value :[1] " Copy of the silver tablet, which the great chief of Kheta, Khetasar, caused to be brought to Pharaoh, by the hand of his messenger, Terteseb, and his messenger, Ramose, to crave peace from the majesty of Ramses II, the Bull of rulers, making his boundary as far as he desires in every land."

" Now at the beginning, since eternity, the relations of the great ruler of Egypt with the great chief of Kheta were, that the God prevented hostilities between them, by treaty. Whereas, in the time of (Muthenra) the great chief of Kheta my brother, he fought w[ith Ramses II], the great ruler of Egypt, yet afterward, beginning with this day, behold Khetasar, the great Chief of Kheta, is in a treaty-relation for establishing the relations which the Re made, and which Sutekh (Hittite) made, for the land of Egypt, with the land of

[1] Br. III, pp. 166-8.

Kheta, in order not to permit hostilities to arise between them, forever." . . . "in order to bring about good peace and good brotherhood between us forever, while he is in brotherhood with me, he is in peace with me ; and I am in brotherhood with him, and I am in peace with him, forever."

. . . "It is better than the former peace and brotherhood which were in the land. . . . The children of the children of the great chief of Kheta shall be in brotherhood and peace with the children of the children of Ramses-Meriamon, etc. . . ." " There shall be no hostilities between them forever. The great Chief of Kheta shall not pass over into the land of Egypt," " forever, to take anything therefrom. Ramses-Meriamon, the great ruler of Egypt, shall not pass over into the land of Kheta, to take anything therefrom, forever. . . ."

The phrases of this earliest known treaty between great monarchs seem to suggest that the political provisions were originally based on the civil, and echo the legal forms used between smaller trespassers.

Good relations must have continued, for they were cemented later by the marriage of Ramses to a Hittite princess, who is portrayed and named on a monument at Abu Simbel, where her father is said to give her away with three subservient addresses to Pharaoh :[1] " Thou didst command the land of Kheta, thou takest captive the people— with all their possessions, the eldest daughter being

[1] Br. III, pp. 182-3, ll. 22-3.

at their head, to [——] before thy beautiful face. Thou commandest them [——] under thy feet forever and ever, together with the whole land of Kheta. While thou shinest upon the throne of Re, every land is under [thy] feet, forever." The name of the princess was Matnefrure. Later her father sent to beg for the aid of an Egyptian god, Khonsu, to heal her younger sister, and the image of the god was sent, and the story of this, corrupted by time, is still an Egyptian folk-tale.

It is not surprising if the rest of Ramses' time, loving as he did to acquire glory, was given to the building of temples and monuments adorned with his story and his deeds. The main scene of work was in northern Egypt, and on the way to the Palestinian frontier. To secure the route he built Per-Atom or Pythom, and Per-Ramassu or Raamses, and probably a connecting chain of forts; but Tanis (Zoan) was the town he favoured most, and indeed transformed by cutting waterways and by raising buildings, with obelisks, temples, and gardens. As the home of his fathers, the Delta was the proper care of this Pharaoh, and yet the most famous of his works is in the far south at Abu Simbel, in Nubia, where he had a great temple to the old trinity of gods Amon, Ra, and Ptah hewn out of the solid rock. It is 200 feet by 100 feet; and 90 feet high, and beside it stands another to Hathor, both having colossal statues 30 feet and 60 feet high, of which six are portraits of the king and the rest of his wife, Nefretiri. It is here that some of the exaggerated scenes of his encounters at Kadesh appear. As Ramses was not really a great conqueror he would not have unlimited supplies of captive labour to draw upon for his works.

The question most interesting to us in Egyptian history—of the relations of these kings to the Israelites—cannot yet be fully answered. There are two main views—one that the Israelites' departure is identical with, or a part of, the expulsion of the Hyksos ; the other that it took place in the reign of Merneptah. The only definite mention of Israel is in the list of peoples subdued by this king, the successor and thirteenth son of Ramses II. They were then classed among such States as Syria and Askalon, and must have been an established and well-known State. Josephus identifies them with the Hyksos, but the entire story of the Old Testament implies the background of a solid, prosperous, and mighty Egypt, trafficking freely with other lands, though possibly suffering other disasters at the time of the Exodus, and the periods of the Eighteenth and Nineteenth Dynasties seem most nearly to correspond with these requirements. That Merneptah himself was the Pharaoh of the Exodus has however been disproved, since his mummy was found at Thebes.

CHAPTER XIV

THE DECLINE

THE main event of Merneptah's reign wa
the first serious invasion of Egypt since th
Hyksos incursion. This was a far mor
widespread movement than that had been ; and
though for the time being it was beaten off, history
cannot but see in it the beginning of the end fo
Egypt.

Merneptah seems to have been occupied in th
second year of his reign in subduing revolt in
Palestine and Syria. He had already been join
ruler with his father for many years, and was a ma
of middle age when Ramses II died ; and no doub
the death of that vain and tyrannical king let loos
the elements of opposition. During these earl
campaigns Merneptah, probably in his third year
encountered and defeated Israel and capture
Gezar ; but while he was occupied in the eas
there was formed against him a great confederac
of far more dangerous foes in the west.

The Libyan semi-nomads and Meshwesh ancestor
of the Berbers, had long been a danger to Egypt
Powerful Pharaohs controlled them, exacted tribute

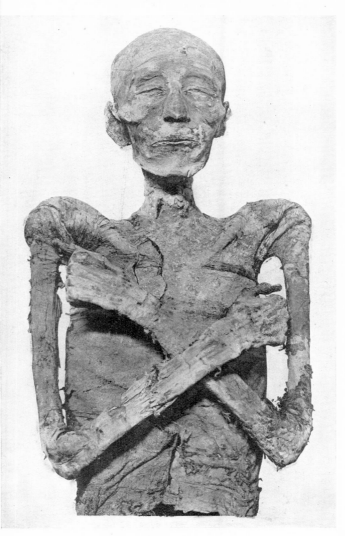

MERNEPTAH

and employed their horsemen as choice cavalry,
but under weaker kings they raided the western
oases almost to Memphis. To these border raiders,
led by an energetic chief named Meryey, were now
added allies who came overseas from the various
southern lands and islands of Europe : Sherden,
probably Sardinians ; Teresh, who may be the
Etruscans ; Shekelesh, possibly Sikili ; Ekwesh,
perhaps Achæans ; and Luka, almost certainly
Lycians from Asia Minor.

Save the Sikels of that early stock called
" Mediterranean Man," all these peoples would
belong to the Nordic folk. It was about 1500 B.C.
that the Nordics began to overflow their settlement on the Carpathians and to spread out in
many directions. They passed southwards in many
successive waves, overrunning Italy, Greece, and
parts of Asia Minor, displacing or overlaying the
earlier and more peaceful stock in these lands, and
the islands about them, with warrior races of a
ruder culture.

The collapse of the Minoan Empire, centred in
Crete, and of the Mycenean culture of Tiryns and
of Troy are incidents in this wide movement, and
in this descent upon Egypt we may sense the far-
flung spray of one wave of their advance, while
about the same period Nordic leaders seem to have
been heading the pressure of other races in western
Europe and to have made their first contact with
the early people of Britain.

Another race which aided in the attack upon

Egypt was the old Hittite enemy ; Merneptah was thus ringed about with foes west, north, and north-eastwards.

It is only from the Egyptian side that we have any details of the struggle, and these, though full, are vitiated by the usual boastful exaggerations, so that Egypt would appear to be completely victorious throughout, whereas in reality her successes were only temporary, and she was gradually forced to relinquish all power over neighbouring lands, until by the reigns of Ramses IX and XI (1100 B.C.) her messengers in the Levant went in danger of their lives.

In the first great encounter Merneptah was able to beat off the confederacy of Libyans and sea-raiders. Egypt [1] " considered not hundreds of thousands in the day of the array." " His infantry marched out, the heavy-armed troops arrived, beautiful in appearance leading the bowmen against every land."

In the following passage it may be recognized that the attack was part of a great racial trek, by the fact that families accompany the warriors : " The wretched fallen chief of Libya, Meryey (Meriai) son of Ded (Tet), has fallen upon the country of Tehenu with his bowmen, . . . Sherden, Shekelesh, Ekwesh, Luka, Teresh, taking the best of every warrior and every man of war of his country. He has brought his wife and his children . . . leaders of the camp, and he has reached the

[1] Br. III, p. 242, ll. 17-19.

western boundary in the fields of Perire " (i.e. a border-town of the Natron district in the Western Delta). . . . They have reached the hills of the oasis " (i.e. The Lesser Oasis, S.W. of the Fayum). Infantry and chariotry in (great) numbers were camped before them (i.e. before the Egyptians) on the shore in front of the district of Perire."[1]

Merneptah, now an old man, showed great vigour in rallying his forces and attacking the host camped on his western frontier. His army was mobilized and in position in about a fortnight, and his attack was well thought out. The Egyptian archery seems to have broken the enemy ranks, and, as they quailed, the Pharaoh loosed his cavalry upon them, sweeping them away and slaughtering them as they fled.

" . . . There was none that escaped among them. Lo, the bowmen of His Majesty spent six hours of destruction among them ; they were delivered to the sword. . . ."[2]   Nine thousand fell, and perhaps as many were taken captive, and among these many were northerners. The leading chief Meryey fled and was disgraced and superseded.

" Lo, as they fought . . . ; the wretched chief of Libya halted, his heart fearing ; withdrew, stopped, knelt, . . . [leaving] sandals, his bow and his quiver in haste behind and everything that was with him . . . his limbs, great terror coursed in his members."

[1] Br. III, p. 243, ll. 1-8.   [2] Br. III, pp. 246-7.

" . . . Lo, the wretched chief of Libya was in speed to flee [by himself] . . ."

" [The commandant] of the fortress of the West [sent] a report to the Court, saying as follows : ' The fallen Meryey has come, his limbs have fled because of his [cowardice], and [he] passed by me, by favour of night, in safety . . . ; he is fallen, and every god is for Egypt."

From the Egyptians' Hymn of Victory we learn that dissension among the Libyans and their allies rendered them harmless for a time :

[1] " The wretched, fallen chief of Libya, fled by favour of night alone, with no plume upon his head, his two feet failed. His women were taken before his face, the grain of his supplies was plundered, and he had no water in the skin to keep him alive. The face of his brother was hostile to slay him, one fought another among his leaders. Their camp was burned and made a roast, all his possessions were food for the troops. When he arrived in his country, he was the complaint of everyone in his land. Ashamed, he bowed himself down, an evil fate removed [his] plume. They all spoke against him, among the inhabitants of his city." . . .

[2] " The kings are overthrown, saying : ' Salâm !
Not one holds up his head among the Nine Bows
Wasted is Tehenu,
Kheta is pacified,
Plundered is Pekanan, with every evil,
Carried off is Askalon,

[1] Br. III, p. 260, 21–28.   [2] Br. III, p. 263, l. 21.

Seized upon is Gezer,
Yenoam is made as a thing not existing.
Israel is desolated, his seed is not ;
Palestine has become a widow for Egypt.
All lands are united, they are pacified ;
Everyone that is turbulent is bound by King
 Merneptah, given life like Re, every day."

An inscription shows that at this time the office
of high priest had become hereditary—as was to
be expected on the final triumph of the cult of
Amon—after the defeat of the Aton-worshippers.

Merneptah thus stayed for a time the oncoming
of disaster to Egypt. He had delivered the country
from the vexatious border-raids and settlement
of strangers along the west ; and the Hymn of
Victory shows how great was the relief the people
experienced, describing men and cattle as straying
out in the fields at will, sitting down happily,
eating their own crops. Evidently the men of
the west had been filtering in by a penetration
not always peaceful, and they had established
themselves especially in the western Delta and
in the oases.

Merneptah reigned for five years after this
victory, and destroyed the fine buildings of
Amenhotep III to provide materials for his own
tomb.

Merneptah was followed by Ramses III, but not
immediately ; for during his and his father's lifetime the power of the throne had been slowly

13

silting down into the hands of officials, priests, and courtiers, and with his death the most formidable among these were rivals for the crown, and succeeded one another rapidly as rulers, until at last complete anarchy and disorder prevailed for a time.

This was ended by a vigorous ruler named Siptah, who was probably of the old kingly line and rallied the more patriotic elements against the Nubian and Syrian influences which had recently prevailed.

Ramses III was his son and owed his peaceful accession to the heavy work his father had achieved in " cleansing the great throne of Egypt and setting in order the entire land ! " But he had to meet very great external dangers, and needed all the resources Egypt could afford him. The northerners from the " isles of the sea " were once more in motion, headed by the Peleset from Crete and the Thekel, possibly Sicilians. These and the allied races Denyen or Danaoi, Sherden, Meshwesh, and Shekelesh were moving in force from Asia Minor through Syria and Palestine. They seem to have broken up the Hittite Empire, and had made a stronghold at Amor, whence they dominated Palestine, while their fleets worked southwards along the coast of the Levant. To meet this threatening flood of northern peoples Ramses could call upon regular levies of native Egyptians for short service and upon the more continuous support of his Libyan, Kehek, and Sherden mercenary cavalry. Archery was still the first arm of the Egyptian array and the decisive factor in battle.

The main mass of the northerners was moving
southwards from the region of the Hittite Empire,
which they had shattered ; but, as in the days of
Ramses II, it was a loose flotilla of sea-raiders
preceding them who first reached Egypt, entering
the Delta mouths, landing on the African coast,
and making common cause with the now reviving
desert tribes. Thus an invasion of Egypt from
the west by these confederates was the first move
in the great offensive. Led by the Libyan chief
Wermer the tribes broke their boundaries and
poured into the country. Ramses came out to
meet them at a frontier post, and secured complete
victory, over 12,000 of the enemy being slain.
Taking advantage of the hill known as " Horns of
the Earth," he built a stronghold to guard the
frontier, and then turned to the yet sterner task
which awaited him in the north-west.

Among the long and inflated descriptions of his
reign found in the inscriptions the following is an
account of this first campaign :[1]

" The land of Temeh is spread out, they flee.
The Meshwesh are hung up in their land,
their plant is uprooted, there is not for them a
survivor. All their limbs tremble for the terror,
which protects (Egyptians) against them.   They
say : ' Behold, we are subject to Egypt, its lord
has destroyed our soul, forever and ever. . . .
Our feet find not a way to go ; we traverse all the
lands as their warriors (mercenaries), they fight

[1] Br. IV, pp. 23–5.

not with us in battle array. . . . The fire has penetrated us, our seed is not. As for Ded, Meshken, Meryey, and Wermer, Themer and every hostile chief who crossed the border of Egypt from Libya, he hath set fire from front to rear. . . . We come to him ; we cry " Salâm " to him, we kiss the ground to his great might . . . King Ramses III.'

" The northern countries are unquiet in their limbs, even the Peleset, the Thekel, who devastate their land, their soul came in the last extremity. They were warriors upon land, also in the sea. Those who came on land . . . Amon-Re was behind them, destroying them ; those who entered into the river-mouths were like wild fowl, creeping into the net. . . . Their hearts fluttered, transported, they were no longer in their bodies. . . . The only lord is in Egypt, no warrior is (so) accurate in shooting, none escapes him . . . the ends of the Great Circle (Okeanos) until they fear with one accord. We will beseech peace, coming with trembling step, for fear of him. . . ."

Preparations were made for the north-western war on an immense scale. The Delta ports were crowded with shipping, and Ramses gathered and equipped hosts of archers, infantry, and chariots in the eastern cities. Leaving a well-fortified frontier behind him, the Pharaoh at last marched into Palestine and swept back the advancing hordes of the enemy as he made his way north. The critical battle of the campaign took place probably in the neighbourhood of Amor, their stronghold, and perhaps the Libyan horsemen played something the same part in it as our own cavalry in the conquest of Palestine. Of this land-campaign there is no coherent account, but it enabled Ramses to claim sovereignty, at least as far as Syria, and to exact tribute from such of the northerners as remained or filtered later into this Amorite region.

The main facts are related by the triumphant Egyptian writer as follows :[1]

" The Countries [i.e. peoples] . . . the Northerners in their isles were disturbed, taken away in the fray at one time. Not one stood before their hands, from Kheta, Kode, Carchemish, Arvad, Alasa [i.e. Cyprus], they were wasted. They set up a camp in one place in Amor. They desolated his people and his land like that which is not. They came with fire prepared before them, forward to Egypt. Their main support was Peleset, Thekel, Shekelesh, Denyen, and Meshwesh. These lands were united and they laid their hands upon the land as far as the circle of the Earth."

At sea Ramses was not less successful. His fleet seems to have followed up the Pharaoh's progress along the coast, and the decisive battle, like so many in ancient history, was fought in harbour, so that the army could engage its archery in aid of the ships. The northerners seem to have been lured unsuspecting into an ambush of the Egyptian fleet and army, to have entered the

[1] Br. IV, pp. 37-8.

harbour, and found it impossible to manœuvre or retire in the presence of the Egyptians. A hail of arrows from ships and from shore pierced them and threw them into such confusion that vessels capsized ; and while sharp-shooters continued to pick off their leaders, the Egyptian ships rammed and pursued the enemy. It speaks well for the spirit and strategy of the Egyptians that they could so thoroughly master enemies whose home was on the sea.

In the following account, which was illustrated by a series of reliefs on the tomb-wall at Medinet Habu in Thebes, " the full flame " is an orientalism for the fleet and " a wall of metal " for the army of Egypt : [1]

" Those who reached my boundary, their seed is not ; their heart and their soul are finished for ever and ever. As for those who had assembled before them on the sea, the full flame was in their front, before the harbour-mouths, and a wall of metal upon the shore surrounded them. They were dragged, overturned and laid low upon the beach ; slain and made heaps from stern to bow of their galleys, while all their things were cast upon the water.

" The Countries (peoples) which came from their isles in the midst of the sea, they advanced to Egypt, their hearts relying upon their arms. The net was made ready for them to ensnare them. Entering stealthily into the harbour-mouth, they

[1] Br. IV, p. 39, ll. 1-7.

fell into it. Caught in their place they were despatched and their bodies stripped. . . . I flourished like a hawk among the fowl, my talons descended upon their heads."[1]

Triumphant as the Hawk-god had proved in these northern campaigns, the force with which he was grappling was too widespread over his whole heaven to be really crushed. Some years of peace and wealth followed, and Ramses seems to have used them well. He improved the organization of his government, classifying his people and securing justice ; while builders were at work to record his deeds at Thebes and his peoples' welfare was furthered by a systematic planting of trees to provide shade. Then the old troubles began to recur : the Meshwesh rose in the far west and once more forced the Libyans across the border. Ramses had in no way relaxed his military guard, and was able to defeat this rising as completely as the first. The story of these years is summarized in the Papyrus Harris :[2] " I made Egypt into many classes consisting of : butlers of the palace, great princes, numerous infantry, and chariotry by the hundred-thousand ; Sherden and Kehek without number ; attendants by the ten-thousand and serf-labourers of Egypt.

" I extended all the boundaries of Egypt ; I overthrew those who invaded them from their lands. I slew the Denyen in their isles, the Thekel and the Peleset were made ashes. The Sherden

[1] Br. IV, p. 45, ll. 22–26.   [2] Br. IV, pp. 200–202.

and the Weshwesh [*sic*] of the sea, they were made as those that exist not, taken captive at one time, brought as captives to Egypt, like the sand of the shore. I settled them in strongholds, bound in my name. Numerous were their classes like hundred-thousands. I taxed them all, in clothing and grain from the storehouses and granaries each year.

" I destroyed the people of Seir, of the tribes of the Shasu, I plundered their tents of their people. . . . I gave them to the gods, as slaves into their houses.

" Behold . . . the Libyans and the Meshwesh were dwelling in Egypt having plundered the cities of the western shore, from Memphis to Kerben. They had reached the great river on both its banks. They it was who plundered the cities of Egwowe during very many years, while they were in Egypt. Behold, I destroyed them, slain at one time. I laid low the Meshwesh, the Libyans, the Esbet, the Keykesh, the Shai, the Hes, and the Beken. . . . I turned them back from trampling the border of Egypt." . . . " I led their cattle into the house of Amon ; they were made for him into herds forever."

Though it is hard to make out the sequence of events from these records, it is evident that Ramses was called again into the north-west by risings of the Bedwin or Shasu tribes, the men of Seir, and also by fresh inroads of the northern settlers into Palestine, so that his great campaigns, though successful, did not really re-establish the old supremacy, and from their close the pressure of the

various peoples upon fertile Egypt grew ever more
irresistible.

Outside pressure, however, has always a tendency
to consolidate the oppressed, and Egypt might yet
have endured had she been sound within. But the
evils which had brought collapse on the death of
Merneptah had been only temporarily controlled
by Siptah and Ramses III. Their revival of the
Empire seems to have been in some respects like
the work of Diocletian and Constantine in the
Roman world. The Court butlers and great
princes were ranged round Pharaoh, as the new
ranks of nobility were ranged by Diocletian ; but
in one case, as in the other, no skill in administration could cut out the real decay, the fact of a military and a priestly caste each sucking the vitality
from the throne. Governors of provinces in the
Delta and in Upper Egypt and Nubia began to
arrogate to themselves such sovereign powers as
that of taxation, the hereditary right to rule, the
power to levy troops. Similarly, the priests, in
the names of the gods, held sway over vast terri-
tories and the great herds of men and beasts who
laboured on them.

Amon of Thebes, as we have seen, had acquired
more and more of supremacy over other gods during
the centuries, and when his prestige was revived
after the interlude of the Aton worship, the hold of
his priests upon all claimants to the throne was
iron. From Harmhab onwards the great Pharaohs
acknowledge their debt to Amon, and pour into his

treasury spoils and captives and all manner of
tribute, so that it is not surprising to find in the
Papyrus Harris that, under Ramses III, Amon
owned nearly 600,000 acres of territory and about
one and a half per cent of the population of Egypt,
while his servants collected directly for him gold
tribute from Nubia, and his wealth was second only
to the king's. The high priesthood too was now
hereditary, and it was virtually impossible for
Pharaoh to withstand the potentate's will. Powerful kings, like Ramses II, might give the priesthood
to a favourite son, but no such powerful kings
succeeded Ramses III, who was forced himself to
depend on foreign nominees at his Court, his
" butlers " and " great princes," sometimes Syrian,
Nubian, or even Lycian strangers. The danger
of such a state showed clearly before his death,
in a harem conspiracy against his life, which
involved many of his foremost courtiers, and in the
rebellion of the vizier, who was besieged in the city
Athribis in the Delta. Over both of these the
king's power triumphed, but they were clear
symptoms of a disease soon to prove fatal.

In the thirty years which followed the death of
Ramses III no less than six short-lived monarchs
followed one another on his throne and bearing
this name, and by the end of their rule Egypt is
seen to have lost her influence upon neighbouring
lands and to be on the verge of breakdown.

The reign of Ramses IX is only notable because
we can see clearly in his tenth year the Pharaoh

setting the high priest of Amon in his own place and authority, for in the reliefs which tell the story the priest's figure is for the first time made equal in size to the king's. In this reign too the flagrant corruption that existed in government is displayed in the records of the trial of certain robbers of the tombs of the Pharaohs, in which it is clear many officials must have been implicated. Another note of the weakness of Egypt in this reign is the fact that a party of Pharaoh's envoys to Syria were held prisoners at Byblos and never returned to Egypt, showing that Syria had quite cast off the yoke.

A paramount power in Palestine was now that of the Philistines. The Hittite power had dissolved, partly through their attacks since Egypt's last contact with it in the reign of Ramses III, and these sea-raiders were now firmly settled on the coastal strip, had swallowed up the Amorite State and split that of Israel into two parts, driving a wedge through them from the sea by the plain of Jezreel to Beth-shean on the Jordan. Beside these Philistines, and akin to them, was a little settlement of the Thekels, their old allies, at a place called Dor on the coast south of Mt. Carmel.

So complete was the decay of the power of Egypt that at the close of the reign of Ramses XI (1118–1090 B.C.) there were two independent kingdoms—that of Hrihor, High-priest of Amon, king of gods, at Thebes ; and that of Smendes, or Nesubenebded, ruling the Delta from Tanis.

In the story of Wenamon glimpses are given of
the state of Egypt at this date and her relations
with the other States. Hrihor, " High-Priest of
Amon and king of gods " is the fully fledged priest-
king whom the rise of Amon's power had foretold,
but he rules only the more southern State and has
very scanty resources. Requiring cedar wood of
Lebanon he sends Wenamon to Syria with a little
money and an image of the god. Wenamon presents
his credentials at Smendes' Court and is allowed to
pass into Syria. He is robbed of his money at Dor,
but confiscates some silver in return ; on reaching
Byblos he is refused permission even to stay, but
the prince, Zakarbaal, finally admits him to an
interview on the prophetic advice of one of his own
attendant youths. Wenamon relates : " I found
him sitting in his upper chamber, leaning his back
against a window, while the waves of the great
Syrian sea were beating against the shore behind
him." Such a clean-cut picture suggests the poetic
quality of the messenger, which perhaps accounts
both for his selection and his final escape. The
whole description is a priceless miniature of the life
of man in these days, before Homer. The argu-
ment between prince and envoy brings out the
complete independence of the former, but shows
that he still admits in theory that Amon is lord ;
and though he repudiates her political control,
he acknowledges Egypt as the source of culture :
" Amon equips all lands ; he equips them having
first equipped the land of Egypt, whence thou

comest. For (craftsmenship) came forth from it to reach my . . . abode ; and teaching came from it to reach my . . . abode. What then are these miserable journeys which they have had thee make ? " Reference is made also to a busy trade with the Delta kingdom : " There are surely twenty ships here in my harbour which are in (connection, traffic) with Nesubenebded ; and at this Sidon, whither thou also wouldest go, there are indeed 10,000 ships also, which are in (connection, traffic) with Berket-El (probably a merchant of Tanis), and sail to his house." Eventually Wenamon gets safely off with his task done, only to be shipwrecked on Cyprus ; but his luck once more revives, and though threatened with death he is able to reach the ruling princess and make his appeal : " The wind drove me to the land of Alasa ; those of the city came forth to me to slay me." Here is a hint of the changed times since the days of the Palace Age of Minoa, when Crete and all the islands were full of unwalled, peaceful, trading towns. " I was brought among them," the story goes on, " to the abode of Heteb, the queen of the city, I said to her : ' If the sea raged, and the wind drove me to the land where I am ; thou wilt not let them take me to slay me ; I being a messenger of Amon. I am one for whom they will seek unceasingly. As for the crew of the prince of Byblos whom they sought to kill, their lord will surely find ten crews of thine and he will slay them on his part.' She had the people called and stationed [before her] ; she said to me : ' Pass the night.' " Here the account lapses, but the fact of its existence on Wenamon's sepulchre proves his final return home.

The story is of immense value, not only for its beauty but for its historic value as a casement through which we can look on the troubled times of transition. Egypt was disintegrating already in this Twentieth Dynasty, and though five more dynasties are recorded it is not natives who rule, but Libyans, Nubians, and finally strangers from the Euphrates valley, till Egypt, in 525 B.C., became a Persian province and so passed, in 332, to Alexander the Great and his satraps, the Ptolemies, and to Rome in 30 B.C.

CHAPTER XV

DISRUPTION

AS the second millennium before Christ drew to a close so did the sway of Egypt over the Old World ; she lost first her place as the leading empire of the Mediterranean lands and then her very existence as a unified and independent State.

The roots of this decay lay in the soil of the Empire itself, with its provinces of north and south sundered by the whole length of the Nile valley ; with its troops of paid tribesmen from Libya and negroes from the Sudan ; and above all its domineering caste of the Amon priesthood, dictating to the Pharaoh himself and setting aside both equity and law in favour of the oracles of their god.

When the last of the Ramses ruled in name it was the high-priest Hrihor who was the acting Pharaoh of Thebes, but the Delta had broken away and installed Nesubenebded as king at Tanis, and neither State could exert authority much beyond its immediate bounds. It was only at the close of his career that Hrihor had reached the throne, and he was quickly followed on it by a son and then a grandson, Paynozem I, who married a granddaughter of Nesubenebded, and so was able to unite the two States and rule for forty years at Tanis. He installed his sons as high-priests at Thebes, but had little authority over them ; and though this Twenty-first Dynasty lasted for a century and a half it could not prevent the disruption which was making separate entities of Kush, Heracleopolis, and the northern kingdoms. From 1090 to about 945 B.C. these Tanites lingered on, and at that time the Hebrews were establishing themselves in the " Promised Land." Led by Joshua and the Judges, they had repeatedly worsted the Canaanites, and had come up against those exiled Cretan warriors of the sea-board whom we know as Philistines.

Against them Saul had led the tribes to victory, and was elected king of the new nation, to be followed by the house of David ; and it is significant of the changed times that their rise coincides with the decay of Egypt. The last king of the Tanite line was Pesibkhenne II, and by his time Egypt had been parcelled out among the leaders of the Libyan troops, set as garrisons on the western cities. In the Twentieth Dynasty these Libyans and Meshwesh had threatened to overrun Egypt, but had been defeated and hurled back into their deserts by Ramses III. For a century they were quiescent, but little by little they had filtered in from the frontier towns to the Nile, holding posts under the Twenty-first Dynasty and occupying city after city, till they rose to the position of satraps of the feeble, priest-ridden Pharaohs.

One such family held Heracleopolis and acquired power over the whole district from Siut to Memphis, and on the death of Pesibkhenne II no force seems to have been needed to enable them to take his place.

Thus a new Libyan dynasty was founded by a chieftain named Sheshonk, and confirmed in its position by the marriage of his son to a daughter of Pesibkhenne II. The new king's control of Egypt was imperfect, for though he followed the recent custom of appointing his son to be High-Priest of Amon at Thebes, he could only administer the country through the hands of his Libyan chiefs, and any such feudal relations have in themselves the risk of rivalry.

Sheshonk was no weakling however, and if the southern States, Nubia and Heracleopolis, were able to assume a measure of independence, his own position at Bubastis was secure, and from that point in the eastern Delta he was able to recover influence in the north. His relations with the princes of Israel are related in the first book of Kings : " Solomon made affinity with Pharaoh king of Egypt, and took Pharaoh's daughter, and brought her into the city of David." (1 Kings iii, 1.) " Pharaoh king of Egypt had gone up, and taken Gezer, and burnt it with fire, and slain the Canaanites that dwelt in the city, and given it

14

for a present unto his daughter, Solomon's wife."
(1 Kings ix, 16.) "Solomon had horses brought out
of Egypt, and linen yarn : the king's merchants
received the linen yarn at a price. And a chariot
came up and went out of Egypt for six hundred
shekels of silver, and a horse for an hundred and
fifty : and so for all the kings of the Hittites, and
for the kings of Syria, did they bring them out by
their means." (1 Kings x, 28, 29.) Solomon was
evidently an important vassal of Egypt, bound by
marriage ties and acting as the agent for Pharaoh,
both in holding the former Canaanite coast-town
and in reopening the valuable Syrian trade-routes.
Sheshonk appears as a monarch both powerful and
wise in making these terms, and they resulted in
the enriching of his treasury with tribute and trade
of the Syrian lands, such as Egypt had not enjoyed
since the days of Amenhotep III. From his
records it is also clear that he had demonstrated
his power in Kush and received a tribute in gold.

When Solomon died and the Hebrew tribes
divided their allegiance, Sheshonk supported
Jeroboam, already a political exile at his Court.
Pharaoh now turned his arms against the house of
David and attacked their city : "It came to pass
in the fifth year of king Rehoboam, that Shishak,
king of Egypt came up against Jerusalem : And
he took away the treasures of the house of the Lord,
and the treasures of the king's house ; he even took
away all ; and he took away all the shields of gold
which Solomon had made." (1 Kings xiv, 25, 26.)

The account in 2 Chron. xii, 3, 4, says further : "And the people were without number that came with him out of Egypt : the Lubims, and the Sukkiims, and the Ethiopians. And he took the fenced cities which pertained to Judah, and came to Jerusalem." Sheshonk commemorated this conquering campaign in a bas-relief at Karnak in two scenes. In the first he appears holding captive by their hair 38 Asiatic chiefs and about to club them to death. In the second he is leading 133 persons, representing captive cities, among the names of which are many places in Judah and Israel, for many resisted Jeroboam even in his own province.

These evidences make it clear that the first Libyan Pharaoh did restore the power and influence of Egypt in Asia, as well as in the Sudan. But the feudal danger of rivalry which he controlled reasserted itself among his successors. The dynasty lingered for over 200 years, but the princes who formed it were of little worth, and city after city preferred its own magnate, until no less than eighteen of these kinglets were ruling in Lower Egypt. The Old Testament witnesses to the weakness of the Libyan kings in the accounts of two expeditions into Palestine in which their armies were worsted. The first seems to have been an effort of Osorkon II, who reigned about 850 B.C., to assert his suzerainty over King Asa of Judea : "And Asa had an army that bare bucklers and spears, out of Judah three hundred thousand ; and out of Benjamin, that bare shields and drew bows, two hundred and fourscore thousand : all these were mighty men of valour. And there came out against them Zerah the Ethiopian with an army of a thousand thousand, and three hundred chariots ; and came unto Mareshah. Then Asa went out to meet him, and they set the battle in array in the valley of Zephathah at Mareshah. . . . So the Lord smote the Ethiopians before Asa, and before Judah ; and the Ethiopians fled. And Asa and the people that were with him pursued them unto Gerar : and there fell of the Ethiopians so many that they could not recover themselves ; for they were destroyed before the Lord, and before his host ; and they carried away very much booty. And they smote all the cities round about Gerar." (2 Chron. xiv, 8-14.) . . . And a later verse asks : " Were not the Ethiopians and the Lubims a huge host, with chariots and horsemen exceeding many ?" (2 Chron. xv, 8.) Civil war between Thebes and Bubastis lasted many years, and the priests of Amon at last took the final step of quitting the royal city and moved away upstream to Napata, the northernmost city of Kush, whence the god had so long drawn his resources in gold.

Meanwhile in the east a new danger was arising to threaten Egypt. By about 1300 B.C. the Semitic tribe, which had settled on the strong height of Assur by the Tigris, were dominating both the upper and lower waters of that river, and began to press westward across the Euphrates and to engage the Aramean peoples of Syria. The struggle between them lasted 600 years, Damascus, the great centre of the Syrian and Hebrew trade-routes, playing a part like that of sixteenth century Venice in repulsing the fierce and merciless eastern invader. At last, in 732 B.C., Damascus itself fell to the arms of Tiglath Pileser III, and the Assyrian power ruled from the Two Rivers to the Mediterranean. Egypt had heard the echo of the fighting, but the only part she seems to have played in it was when Takelot II, one of the Libyan Pharaohs, sent a contingent of 1,000 men to join the Hebrew and Aramean forces against Shalmaneser II. This was a contemptible force for Egypt to raise, and shows how far she was already fallen. The coalition met the Assyrian's armies at Qarqar on the Orontes River and were completely shattered. Egypt continued to disintegrate under the so-called Twenty-third and Twenty-fourth Dynasties, and neither Pedibast, who ruled at Bubastis at the time of the fall of Damascus, nor his successors, Osorkon III, and Takelot III, could check the decay.

The priesthood of Amon had acted shrewdly in their own interests as usual in moving their head-quarters from the turbulent northern State up to Kush, where there were none to rival their authority and resources. Little is known of the internal history of this region. Napata lay just below the fourth cataract, and some 300 miles above was the island and town of Meroë, half-way between the fifth and sixth cataracts; beyond lay the mysteries and treasures of the tropical interior. Here, in Napata, now arose the new kingdom of Amon in the land of the Ethiopians. Men of mixed Egyptian and negroid race came to hold all the titles of Pharaoh and under the dictation of the priests to claim the lordship of the Two Lands. In 721 B.C. the king was a Nubian, and the priests of Amon were not ashamed to hold office under this southerner and to pay him all the honours of the ancient Pharaohs. The next step was for him to attempt the recovery of the northern valley. There the rivalry of the States had reached an acute stage, a prince Tefnakht of Sais in the western Delta making head against the authority of Osorkon III of Bubastis, and securing the submission of the Delta and Nile cities till he had advanced to Hermopolis, half-way to Thebes. There the daughter of Osorkon was priestess of Amon, with a nominal authority over the region, but the Nubian Pharaoh, Piankhi, suddenly appeared with strong forces which had enabled him to pass through Thebes and attack Hermopolis. Tefnakht was driven in flight before him and the victorious Ethiopian seized city after city. His greatest exploit was the capture of Memphis, which Tefnakht had counted impregnable. Built on the west bank it was strongly fortified on the land side, and on the east protected by the waters of the Nile, here artificially raised so that the ships rode level with the houses. Piankhi showed his generalship by taking advantage of this very feature : his ships assailed the anchored

boats, mastered them, and then made of them a
quay by which the troops could reach and scale the
walls. Memphis was surprised with little fighting,
and the news of its downfall sent the fear of the
Nubian into all the cities of the Delta. Piankhi
now marched on to Heliopolis and was hailed as
Lord of Egypt in the ancient sanctuary of the
sun-god there, receiving the homage of Osorkon ;
and then advancing to Athribis, where all the Delta
chiefs submitted to him, even Tefnakht sending
a humble message, though he was careful not to
yield his person to the conqueror. Thus the
Ethiopian monarch had made good his claim to be
the unrivalled Lord of the Two Lands. He returned " triumphant " as the old Pharaohs, leaving
his sister-consort installed as priestess at Thebes.
His hold on the north, however, was not thorough,
for Osorkon III, and after him Tefnakht's son,
Bocchoris, held sway in Thebes. Consequently,
on Piankhi's death his brother, Sabaka, succeeding,
found it necessary to demonstrate his authority
over Lower Egypt. He completely subdued the
princes of the Delta, and Bocchoris, according to
Manetho, suffered death by burning. Shabaka
further showed his strength in the internal affairs
of his kingdom, and lessened the overweening power
of the Amon priests, reinstating his sister at Thebes.
He left his crown to a son, Shabataka ; but a
claimant with perhaps better rights soon appeared
in Piankhi's son, Taharka, a prince who had already
led the Nubian armies against a mortal enemy.

For during this period of the Nubian ascendancy, the danger from Assyria had been constantly waxing. Since the defeat at Qarqar in 854 B.C. several revolts in Palestine had only resulted in drawing the Assyrians further and further into the land to take reprisals. In 722 B.C. Sargon II had captured Samaria and carried Israel into captivity ; two years later he suppressed a fresh rising and marched to the very frontiers of Egypt.

It was in 711 B.C. that the Nubian Shabaka attempted to form a coalition to resist this eastern danger. Philistia, Moab, and Edom joined him, and Judah, despite the warnings of Isaiah, also intrigued with Egypt. Sargon II however gave them no time to act, and it was not until the reign of his son, Sennacherib, that the alliance matured. Shabaka's levies were commanded by Taharka and advanced to meet Sennacherib, who had subdued all the coast cities but Tyre and was encamped by Askalon. His disciplined Assyrian soldiery easily shattered the coalition, and meanwhile other contingents were besieging Hezekiah in Jerusalem and ravaging his country. It was not " the staff of the bruised reed," Egypt, but " the act of God," in the form of a mortal attack of malaria, that defeated and slew the Assyrian host ; "and when men arose early in the morning, behold, they were all dead corpses." After this defeat Taharka seems to have retired to Nubia ; possibly Pharaoh's censure followed him and made him angry, for he next appears with an army, prepared to wrest the kingdom from Shabaka's son. He defeated and slew Shabataka and set up his own throne at Tanis. Taharka's career proves him to have been the strongest Pharaoh of his house : He ruled undisturbed for over a decade until in Assyria Esarhaddon had displaced his father, Sennacherib, and revived the war policy against Egypt on a more systematic scale than ever before. Taharka was not unaware of the menace, and succeeded in beating back the first attack in the year 673 B.C. He then made alliance with Tyre, but in 670 B.C. Esarhaddon returned and, after capturing the Phœnician city, pressed on right into Egypt. At Memphis the Nubian made his stand, but in vain ; the Ninevites entered and spoiled the city. Pharaoh still escaped, and though all the Delta chiefs submitted, it was only until the conqueror had departed, cutting the record of his conquests on the rock face at Beirut beside that of Ramses II, and again in Syria. Invited by the cities of the Delta, Taharka at once resumed his rule, and Esarhaddon died before he could inflict fresh chastisement. His son Ashurbanipal took up the work, and his generals routed Taharka at Karbanit below Memphis, and followed in pursuit to Thebes. The close of the campaign was the signal for fresh intrigues, but this time the enemy were alert and the rebels were sent captive to Nineveh. Among them was Necho, lord of Sais and descendant of Tefnakht, and this prince contrived to ingratiate himself with the Assyrian and was sent back to his dominions as deputy. Taharka's star was setting, and in 663 B.C. he died, leaving Tanutamon, a son of Shabaka, on the throne. This prince made a successful effort to regain Lower Egypt and held Memphis, but only to invite the final disaster. Ashurbanipal's fresh armies drove him out, marched upon Thebes, and at last the great city of the Pharaohs fell a prey to the eastern stranger. On their departure Tanutamon re-entered Thebes for a few days, but after 654 B.C. his place knows him no more and no Ethiopian again attempts to recover Egypt.

Contact between the northern and southern valleys seems to have gradually ceased, and Kush is lost to civilization for a time. Even Napata seems to have been thought too much exposed to attack, and the Ethiopian government moved its seat to Meroë (or Barua), seventy miles south of the confluence of the Atbara River with the Nile. A town had existed there from the eighth century B.C., as is shown by the ruins of a Twelfth Dynasty cemetery and two huge brick mastabas. Meroë lies at the opening of a fertile *khor*, or gorge, by which a natural trade-route leads across the desert to the Atbara River, and which thus formed a direct channel to the traffic of the Red Sea and India. Recent excavations have shown that it was a populous city, with temples to Amon and the sun. The latter, which was at the entrance to the gorge, was probably the original " Table of the Sun " described by Herodotus. Sculpture from the temple of Amon shows a figure of the king, with an Egyptian

THE SUN TEMPLE AT MEROË

type of face, kneeling before Horus, while behind a high-priest makes offerings. Thus it is clear that the priests when they left Thebes carried the old traditions and ritual on in their new southern kingdom.

CHAPTER XVI

REVIVAL AND COLLAPSE

THE story of Egypt seemed to have ended with its conquest by Ashurbanipal, but a curious temporary revival afterwards took place, like the clear flaming of a light that precedes its extinction.

Necho of Sais had ended his life in a struggle with Tanutamon, and his son Psamtik had been forced to take refuge with his father's suzerain at Nineveh. As a loyal vassal he was restored by the Assyrian arms to his patrimony at Sais, and used this protected vantage ground as a means to making himself independent lord of Lower Egypt. It was a fortunate moment, for the Assyrians were preoccupied in wars with Babylon and with the new forces arising in Cilicia and on their northern frontiers. Psamtik was thus able to secure control of the cities about him and to advance upon Thebes without correction, possibly even representing himself as the Assyrian agent in this conquest. The forces which he employed were not merely the Libyan troops, for many of these served his feudal rivals in the Delta, but regiments of Carian and

Ionian Greeks, who had come to him from the camp
of his ally in Asia Minor, King Gyges of Lydia.
These Greek barbarian tribes had long been pouring
over the Balkans and across the Hellespont, and
had been occasionally employed as mercenaries by
the Pharaohs since the days of the Empire. It
was by their means that the vassals and neighbours
of Assyria now hoped to build up a rampart against
her cruel westward pressure, and in this attempt
Lydia and Cilicia were as much concerned as
Palestine and Egypt. Psamtik balanced the disloyal tendencies of his Libyan and Egyptian
feudatories with the weight of these disciplined
mercenary Greeks—much as our later Saxon kings
used Norse or Norman levies—and for a time this
policy succeeded.

Psamtik differed from his predecessors in outlook
as well as in origin. The position of Sais was not
central like that of Thebes : it lay on a western
branch of the Nile mouths and looked to the
Mediterranean rather than to Egypt proper.
Psamtik himself, too, had shared the adventures
of his father, Necho, and had himself experienced
life at the foreign Court. His outlook was away
from Egypt to the new world of intercourse between
East and West ; he recognized that the true
interests of his throne lay in sharing in the trade
and progress of the coming age. He encouraged
Greek merchants as well as mercenaries to settle
in Egypt, and the wisdom and wonders of the
Nile land began to be noised abroad among the

seventh-century Greeks. Once he had subdued his feudal rivals, Psamtik allowed the more trustworthy of them to retain their cities ; but his power remained supreme in the Delta, and under him Northern Egypt was able to live peaceably and to revive the old plenty and beauty which belonged of right to her diligent and unaggressive peasantry. It was a real renaissance which she now enjoyed. Together with the new trading adventures and new foreign influences came a passionate revival of the old traditions and religious ceremonies ; and whereas it was only the rulers who appreciated the former, the whole patient people rejoiced to revive the feasts and adorn the temples of the ancient gods of the Golden Age of the Empire. The " Book of the Dead " was revised, as the priests diligently studied the archaic language, which none but themselves now understood. The arts of painting and carving had never died out, but they flourished freely again at this time ; and though the motives employed were copies of the old work, new skill was displayed in some examples. Since the Nubian period a popular form of writing— the Demotic—had become common, being a cursive script, while only the priests and scholars continued to read or write the hieroglyphic. The priesthood was hereditary, and religion tended to become more and more a rigid cult of magical ritual—the worship of Osiris and Isis taking the foremost place.

The reign of Psamtik thus marks a definite stage

in the decay of Egypt; for though a time of prosperity and revival, it was marked by that tendency to retrospection that comes upon a people nearing their end as it does upon the individual : Egypt looked back even while her rulers looked forward. After half a century of steady government Psamtik was peaceably succeeded by his son, Necho. He took in hand at once a campaign against Palestine, for which his father had already cleared the way by the capture of Ashdod after a siege sustained for several years. The intercourse with Greek pirates and Tyrian sailors had borne its fruit, and Pharaoh Necho had fleets in the Red Sea as well as the Mediterranean and quickly mastered the coasts of Philistine, Gaza, and Askalon. The Saite monarch now marched into Palestine with a great host, and King Josiah of Judah made an attempt to repulse him in the Kishon valley at Megiddo. The Egyptian armies had not been gathered against him but against his Assyrian lord, and the story in 2 Chron. xxxv, 21, tells of Necho's protest : "What have I to do with thee, thou king of Judah ? I come not against thee this day, but against the house wherewith I have war : and the God hath commanded me to hasten : forbear thee from meddling with the God, who is with me, that he destroy thee not." Nevertheless, Josiah would not turn his face from him. . . And the archers shot at King Josiah ; and the king said to his servants : " Have me away ; for I am sore wounded . . . and he died." (2 Chron. xxxv, 23, 24.)

Pharaoh Necho passed on after this against Assyria, but he met no opposition in Syria ; and even when he reached the banks of the Euphrates there was still no array of the enemy to contest his passage. Assyria's hour was come. In Psamtik's reign there had descended from the mountains that screen the steppes of Russia on to the plateau of Asia Minor a horde of Scythians ravaging all her northern frontiers ; simultaneously from the north-east, beyond the Caspian, had trekked the Iranian tribes, another branch of these nomad grasslanders led by the Medes and Persians. Soon after 700 B.C. the kingdom of the Medes was formed on Assyria's north-east flank, menacing Nineveh across the Tigris ; meanwhile from the south came a fresh troop of nomad Semites, called Kaldi, to occupy the site of fallen Babylon and re-erect it. From all sides these vigorous young peoples now impinged upon Assyria, and by the middle of the century her strength was sapped in struggling with them. Thus she was helpless to oppose the advance of Pharaoh Necho to the Euphrates, and he was able to display the might of the new Egypt to the very confines of the old Empire. Could he have crossed the 200 miles between the rivers he might have joined the ring of foes that in two years' time overthrew Nineveh ; but for that he was not prepared, and when he had recorded his advance to Naharina he turned homewards. On his way he took Josiah's successor, Jehoahaz, and " put him in bands at Ribleh in the land of Hamath, that

he might not reign at Jerusalem ; and put the land
to a tribute of an hundred talents of silver, and a
talent of gold. And Pharaoh Necho made Eliakim
the son of Josiah king in the room of Josiah his
father, and turned his name to Jehoiakim, and
took Jehoahaz away : and he came to Egypt and
died there." (2 Kings xxiii, 33, 34.) Over this
exile Jeremiah spoke the prophetic lament : " Weep
ye not for the dead . . . but weep sore for him that
goeth away : for he shall return no more, nor see
his native country. . . . He shall not return
thither any more : but in the place whither they
have led him captive, there shall he die, and he
shall see this land no more " (Jer. xxii, 10–12)—
a word true, not for this king alone, but for how
many millions of his scattered people even to our
own day !

It was at this point that Nineveh was taken
and the great Assyrian Empire divided between
the conquering Medes and the Chaldeans, so that
it was from the new masters of Babylon that
Egypt had to expect the chastisement of her
audacity. It came swiftly, Nebuchadnezzar, son
of the conqueror, gathering a host to recover the
western provinces. Necho, with characteristic boldness, decided to meet the danger half-way, and led
his Greek and Egyptian forces once more to the
Euphrates. Jeremiah chanted of the world-shaking
event : " Who is this that riseth up like the Nile,
whose waters toss themselves like the rivers ?
Egypt riseth up like the Nile, and his waters toss

themselves like the rivers ; and he saith, I will rise up, I will cover the earth ; I will destroy the city and the inhabitants thereof. Go up, ye horses ; and rage, ye chariots ; and let the mighty men go forth ; Cush and Put, that handle the shield ; and the Lubim, that handle and bend the bow." (Jer. xlvi, 7–9.) There at Carchemish the fate of Egypt was settled : " They stood not, because the Lord did drive them. He made many to stumble, yea, they fell one upon another : and they said (being hirelings), Arise, and let us go again to our own people, and to the land of our nativity, from the oppressing sword. They cried there, Pharaoh king of Egypt is but a noise ; he hath let the appointed time pass by. . . . Egypt is a very fair heifer, but destruction out of the North is come ; it is come. Also her hired men in the midst of her are like calves of the stall ; for they also are turned back, they are fled away together ; they did not stand ; for the day of their calamity is come upon them, the time of their visitation." (Jer. xlvi, 15–17 ; 20, 21.)

Nebuchadnezzar pursued the rout from Carchemish into Palestine, where Jehoiakim, Necho's puppet, at once submitted ; but his own accession recalled him suddenly to Babylon, so Egypt was allowed to make terms, relinquishing all claim to the Asiatic provinces, and Necho ended his days in quiet : " And the king of Egypt came not again any more out of his land : for the king of Babylon had taken from the brook of Egypt (El Arish) unto the river Euphrates all that pertained to the king of Egypt." (2 Kings xxiv, 7.)

Necho resigned himself to the inevitable and turned to the development of the resources of his own land. He set to work to clear the ancient canal between the eastern arms of the Nile and the Red Sea. Herodotus tells (Book II, Chap. 158): " This prince was the first to attempt the construction of the canal to the Red Sea—a work completed afterwards by Darius the Persian—the length of which is four days' journey and the width such as to admit of two triremes being rowed along it abreast."

Necho's son, Psamtik II, did little of note beyond an expedition into Nubia, but his successor, Hophre, or Apries, was more active : he stirred up revolt in which Zedekiah of Judah was the central figure supported by Tyre, Sidon, Moab, and Ammon. Apries, however, instead of consolidating this coalition, wrecked it by attacking the Phœnician cities ; so that Nebuchadnezzar, taking up a post of vantage on the Orontes, was able to deal with Judah at his ease. Jerusalem fell in the year 586 B.C. and Tyre in 573. Apries, however, escaped, and Egypt enjoyed a respite till the end of his reign. He was superseded by one of his own generals, Ahmose, whom he had sent to put down a mutiny of the Egyptian troops, provoked apparently by jealousy of the Greek mercenaries and a recrudescence of national feeling, which it was easy for the Egyptian general to turn to his own account. But even

16

Ahmose could not " put the clock back," and though he made some show of restricting the foreigner to the new city of Naucratis, his whole reign shows him obliged to continue the cosmopolitan tendencies of his predecessors. No king of Egypt had more close relations with the Greeks than he. Herodotus gives a fuller account of him than of any other Pharaoh, and we see him hard at work organizing the trade, with Naucratis playing the part of a staple town. He made careful enquiry into the economic resources of his land, and every Egyptian was obliged to make an annual statement of his means of livelihood. This law was adopted by Solon when he visited Egypt and applied by him to the city-State of Athens ; Herodotus commends it as a wise measure. Ahmose, with his foreign interests, was not afraid to make the priests pay their share of the burdens of the State, and was possibly not sorry in this way to reduce their importance. He had relations too with the Cyrenians and with the King of Samos, Polycrates. He joined a coalition of the western powers, in which Lydia was the chief, to resist the Persian power. The Medes had been overthrown and Persia was threatening to overrun all Asia, when Egypt and Sparta joined Lydia. But Cyrus moved with such speed that Lydia fell before they could make a move, and Babylon proved equally powerless. Thus the oncoming fate of Egypt was clear to see before Ahmose died. The short-lived renaissance which the Saite kings had effected had

no roots in the old Egyptian past : it was rather a
sucker than an offshoot of the parent stem.

Cyrus of Persia was succeeded by his son
Cambyses, and in the year 525 B.C. this king under-
took the conquest of Egypt.   Herodotus says that
he made a treaty with the ruler of the Arabian
tribes to supply his forces with water for the passage
of the desert.   Ahmose's son, Psamtik III, had
just succeeded to the throne of Egypt and met the
Persian invader on his eastern frontier ; he was
there defeated and forced to flee to Memphis.   The
Persian sent a herald to demand submission, but
he was torn to pieces by the Memphites, and to
avenge him Cambyses advanced, captured the
city, and sacked it.   All Egypt, including Libya
and Cyrene, then submitted.   Pharaoh was for a
time honourably treated, but soon accused of
intrigue and forced to slay himself.   Cambyses
now planned great conquests, to include Carthage,
Kush, and Meroë, but failed to prosecute them :
the attack on the Phœnicians was abandoned, an
expedition against the Oasis was swallowed up by
sandstorms ; and the army sent against Kush
starved for want of supplies and was easily destroyed by the troops of Nastasen of Meroë.   From
this time Cambyses seems to have become insane,
and his actions outraged all the religious as well as
the national feeling of the Egyptians, for he dese-
crated the temples and wounded the sacred Apis
bull.   Finally he fell by his own hand as he returned
towards Susa.   Darius, on the contrary, ruled well

in Egypt as elsewhere, venerating the ancient gods, founding a college for priests at Sais and a temple to Amon in the Oasis, developing the country's resources, and achieving the completion of the great canal.

His successors, Xerxes and Artaxerxes, on the other hand, cared little for the traditions of Egypt ; and by the close of the fifth century B.C. the Persian rule had become so weak and so detested that the Egyptians managed for a time to shake it off, and native princes held sway in one city and another, forming the so-called Twenty-eighth to Thirtieth Dynasties. The strongest of these kinglets, although the last, was Nectanebos, who reigned seventeen years ; but in 340 B.C. Egypt became once more a province of the Persian Empire of Artaxerxes III (Ochus), who had recaptured Pelusium and thence subdued the land. Thus when the famous Alexander of Macedon ended the century-old struggle of Greeks and Persians by the defeat of Darius III at Issus, Egypt was one of the provinces of Persia that fell to his sword. The Persian satrap could make no resistance, and Alexander was admitted to Memphis as its lord. He assumed the usual titles and sacrificed to the Egyptian gods, later visiting the Temple of Amon (now also called Zeus, or Jupiter) to consult the oracle. His seal was set upon the country for all time by the founding of his city, Alexandria, with its magnificent double harbour, opposite to, and soon to include, the Homeric isle of Pharos.

By its means he would draw the traffic of east and west along a southern route to rival the old trade of Tyre and make Greek merchandise supreme. Greeks and Jews flocked into the emperor's new city, and it quickly became a centre not only of trade but of learning, and the most cosmopolitan scene of the new age.

At Alexander's death in 323 B.C. Egypt passed under the real guidance of his general Ptolemy Lagus, who, after the short and nominal reigns of Philip III and Alexander IV, stepped on to the throne of the Pharaohs and founded a dynasty to endure for two and a half centuries. He was one of the best rulers Egypt ever had, giving the people peace and opportunity for progress ; it was he who founded the great Library of Alexandria, to be one of the purest fountains of learning for rising Europe through nearly three centuries. But Ptolemy's rule was, after all, the final stage in the Graecizing of Egypt, and with her new population of immigrants from the Ægean and from Syria she turns at last definitely to face the West and to play her part in the dispersion of Hebrew faith and Greek philosophy among the younger western lands. Aristotle had bidden Alexander, when he entered Egypt, " to be a ruler to the Hellenes and a master to the barbarians, to provide for the former as friends and comrades, to use the latter like animals or plants," and it was on these lines that the rule of the Ptolemies proceeded. Jewish merchants had settled at Elephantine and in many of the other great cities, and the favoured Greeks were every-where, their language in general use among the educated. These tendencies grew under Ptolemy II, who built the Pharos lighthouse, one of the Seven Wonders of the Greek World, as well as the new towns of Berenice and Arsinoë.

It was not until this reign that the first history of Egypt was written by the Egyptian Manetho, little of which beyond the list of kings has survived, but which has been a priceless clue to the unravelling of many problems. At the same time cunning scribes sent by the high-priest Eleazer from Jeru-salem helped to draw up the translation of the Hebrew Scriptures, known as the Septuagint. The Library is said at this time to have contained 300,000, or even 700,000 volumes.

In 196 B.C. Ptolemy III succeeded. Like his fathers he was careful to cultivate the support of the priesthood, and they rewarded him with eulogies set up in all the temples. One such stele is the famous Rosetta stone, deciphered by Cham-pollion—the key to the reading of the Egyptian hieroglyphic script. Egypt was being more and more exploited as well as developed by the foreigner, and under the later Ptolemies it has been said that " the Egyptian toiled chiefly for other lands." Ptolemy XIII came to the throne in 80 B.C., and the heavy taxation which he laid upon the people led to a revolt before which he fled to demand aid from Rome. His appeal was for a time disregarded, but in 55 B.C. Gabinius, Roman governor of Syria, reinstated him, thus giving to the Republic her first real hold on Egypt. Since 168 B.C. Rome had indeed enjoyed a nominal suzerainty; in 81 B.C. Alexander II had formerly bequeathed his kingdom to the Republic, and from that time the Romans had extorted large sums from the Ptolemy, which he could only raise by laying unbearable taxes upon the people. The young Ptolemy XIV had as consort his sixteen-year-old sister, Cleopatra, in accordance with Egyptian usage, but he and his ministers combined to deny her all power, and she was driven from the Court.

At this juncture Pompey, in flight from Cæsar, anchored off the coast and was betrayed and murdered by Ptolemy's orders. Cæsar, arriving in pursuit, spurned his rival's butchers and summoned Ptolemy before him. Cleopatra meanwhile had made her way to Cæsar's presence and had secured his favour. Their alliance, despite the nominal reconciliation of the king and queen, alarmed the Alexandrians and occasioned the outburst of revolt, in which the Roman troops long stationed in Egypt joined. Hemmed in the palace and eastern harbour Cæsar was in real danger of being cut off from reinforcements and needed all his skill and valour to recover Pharos and secure victory. For six, or probably nine, months he remained with Cleopatra, ignoring Roman concerns, and seems to have contemplated an empire of east and west for which Egypt, with her rich cornlands and her harbour of Berenice on the Red

Sea, should be the stepping-stone. Ptolemy had perished in the revolt, and his younger brother had replaced him as king and consort ; but when Cæsar left Egypt and her son Cæsarion was born, Cleopatra followed to Rome, where she witnessed his triumph and his tragic death in 44 B.C. In Egypt he had been hailed as an incarnation of Amon and Cæsarion legitimatized as heir to the throne of Egypt, if not to the government of Rome. To clear his path, Cleopatra compassed the death of her young brother, and at seventeen Cæsarion was declared of age and co-regent with her.

Meanwhile Cleopatra had been called to task by Marc Anthony for siding with Brutus and appeared before his judgment-seat at Tarsus. Henceforth he was her captive and lifelong slave.

It was his support of her challenge to Octavius to yield the empire to Cæsarion that led Anthony to the final campaign, and the flight of her galleys entraining his own that turned the fortune of the day at Actium. They fled to Egypt, only to be followed by Octavius ; and with his attack on Alexandria, first Anthony and then the queen committed suicide. They were buried together in the tomb of the Ptolemies, and the queen's son Cæsarion was executed. Egypt became an integral part of the new empire ruled directly by Augustus, and under him a storehouse of corn and funds for the imperial city. " Not 20 Egyptian ships in the year ventured forth under the Ptolemies from the Arabian Gulf ; now 120 merchantmen annually

sail to India from the port of Myos Hermos alone,"
so wrote a contemporary of the first emperor's
work in clearing the Egyptian seas of pirates. So
the fortunes of Egypt were finally wrapped up in
those of the great world-embracing empire, and her
independent existence merged in the civilizations
she had helped to rear.

CHRONOLOGY.

B.C. 3500 TO A.D.

B.C.
3500 —

— 3400 Menes
        Dyn. I

3000 — — 2980 Dyn. III
        — 2900 Dyn. IV   Pyramid Age

        — 2750 Dyn. V

        — 2625 Dyn. VI

2500 — — 2475 ⌐

                    Feudal Period

        — 2160 ⌊

2000 — — Dyn. XII

        — 1780 Hyksos Period

        — 1580 Dyn. XVIII
1500 — — 1501 Thutmose III
        — 1375 Ikhnaton   Empire
        — 1350 Tutenkhamon
        — 1292 Ramses II
        — 1200 Dyn. XX

        — 1090 Dyn. XXI
1000 —
        — 945 Dyn. XXII
                (Libyan)

        — 712 Dyn. XXV
                (Nubian)

500 — — 525 Cambyses
                (Persian)
        — 333 Alexander
        — 323 Ptolemy

A.D. — — 31 Rome

INDEX

Printed by Jarrold & Sons, Limited, Norwich, England

A SELECTION FROM

MESSRS. METHUEN'S PUBLICATIONS

This Catalogue contains only a selection of the more important books published by Messrs. Methuen. A complete catalogue of their publications may be obtained on application.

Armstrong (W. W.). THE ART OF CRICKET. *Second Edition. Cr. 8vo. 6s. net.*

Bain (F. W.).—
A DIGIT OF THE MOON : A Hindoo Love Story. THE DESCENT OF THE SUN : A Cycle of Birth. A HEIFER OF THE DAWN. IN THE GREAT GOD'S HAIR. A DRAUGHT OF THE BLUE. AN ESSENCE OF THE DUSK. AN INCARNATION OF THE SNOW. A MINE OF FAULTS. THE ASHES OF A GOD. BUBBLES OF THE FOAM. A SYRUP OF THE BEES. THE LIVERY OF EVE. THE SUBSTANCE OF A DREAM. *All Fcap. 8vo. 5s. net.* AN ECHO OF THE SPHERES. *Wide Demy 8vo. 10s. 6d. net.*

Baker (C. H. Collins). CROME. Illustrated. *Quarto. £5, 5s. net.*

Balfour (Sir Graham). THE LIFE OF ROBERT LOUIS STEVENSON. *Twentieth Edition. In one Volume. Cr. 8vo. Buckram, 7s. 6d. net*

Bateman (H. M.). A BOOK OF DRAWINGS. *Fifth Edition. Royal 4to. 10s. 6d. net.* MORE DRAWINGS. *Second Edition. Royal 4to. 10s. 6d. net.* ADVENTURES AT GOLF. *Demy 4to. 7s. 6d. net.*

Belloc (H.).—
PARIS, 8s. 6d. net. HILLS AND THE SEA, 6s. net. ON NOTHING AND KINDRED SUBJECTS, 6s. net. ON EVERYTHING, 6s. net. ON SOMETHING, 6s. net. FIRST AND LAST, 6s. net. THIS AND THAT AND THE OTHER, 6s. net. ON, 6s. net. MARIE ANTOINETTE, 18s. net. THE PYRENEES. 8s. 6d. net.

Blackmore (S. Powell). LAWN TENNIS UP-TO-DATE. Illustrated. *Demy 8vo. 12s. 6d. net.*

Butler (Kathleen T.). A HISTORY OF FRENCH LITERATURE. *Two Vols. Each Cr. 8vo. 10s. 6d. net.*

Campbell (Olwen Ward). SHELLEY AND THE UNROMANTICS. *Demy 8vo. 16s. net.*

Chandler (Arthur), D.D., late Lord Bishop of Bloemfontein—
ARA CŒLI : An Essay in Mystical Theology, 5s. net. FAITH AND EXPERIENCE, 5s. net. THE CULT OF THE PASSING MOMENT, 6s. net. THE ENGLISH CHURCH AND REUNION, 5s. net. SCALA MUNDI, 4s. 6d. net.

Chesterton (G. K.).—
THE BALLAD OF THE WHITE HORSE. ALL THINGS CONSIDERED. TREMENDOUS TRIFLES. ALARMS AND DISCURSIONS. A MISCELLANY OF MEN. THE USES OF DIVERSITY. FANCIES VERSUS FADS. *All Fcap. 8vo. 6s. net.* WINE, WATER, AND SONG. *Fcap. 8vo. 1s. 6d. net.*

Clutton-Brock (A.)—
WHAT IS THE KINGDOM OF HEAVEN ? *Fifth Edition. Fcap. 8vo. 5s. net.* ESSAYS ON ART. *Second Edition. Fcap. 8vo. 5s. net.* ESSAYS ON BOOKS. *Third Edition. Fcap. 8vo. 6s. net.* MORE ESSAYS ON BOOKS. *Fcap. 8vo. 6s. net.* SHAKESPEARE'S HAMLET. *Fcap. 8vo. 5s. net.* SHELLEY: THE MAN AND THE POET. *Second Edition, Revised. Fcap. 8vo. 7s. 6d. net.*

Conrad (Joseph). THE MIRROR OF THE SEA : Memories and Impressions. *Fourth Edition. Fcap. 8vo. 6s. net.*

Dark (Sidney) and Grey (Rowland). W. S. GILBERT : His Life and Letters. Illustrated. *Second Edition. Demy 8vo. 15s. net.*

Dolls' House (The Queen's). THE BOOK OF THE QUEEN'S DOLLS' HOUSE. Vol. I. THE QUEEN'S DOLLS' HOUSE. Edited by A. C. BENSON, C.V.O., and SIR LAWRENCE WEAVER, K.B.E. Vol. II. THE QUEEN'S DOLLS' HOUSE LIBRARY. Edited by E. V. LUCAS. Illustrated. *Crown 4to. £3, 3s. net, each.*

Drever (James). THE PSYCHOLOGY OF EVERYDAY LIFE. *Fourth Edition. Cr. 8vo. 6s. net.* THE PSYCHOLOGY OF INDUSTRY. *Cr. 8vo. 5s. net.*

Dutt (W. A.). A GUIDE TO THE NORFOLK BROADS. Illustrated. *Demy 8vo. 6s. net.*

Edwardes (Tickner). THE LORE OF THE HONEY-BEE. *Tenth Edition. Cr. 8vo. 7s. 6d. net.* THE BEE-MASTER OF WARRILOW. *Third Edition. Cr. 8vo. 7s. 6d. net.* BEE-KEEPING FOR ALL : A Manual of Honeycraft. *Cr. 8vo. 3s. 6d. net.*

Einstein (A.). RELATIVITY : THE SPECIAL AND THE GENERAL THEORY. Translated by ROBERT W. LAWSON. *Eighth Edition. Cr. 8vo. 5s. net.* SIDELIGHTS ON RELATIVITY. Two Lectures by ALBERT EINSTEIN. *Cr. 8vo. 3s. 6d. net.* THE MEANING OF RELATIVITY. *Second Edition. Cr. 8vo. 5s. net.*
Other Books on the Einstein Theory.
SPACE—TIME—MATTER. By HERMANN WEYL. *Demy 8vo. 18s. net.* THE PRINCIPLE OF RELATIVITY. By ALBERT EINSTEIN, H. A. LORENTZ, H. MINKOWSKI, and H. WEYL. With notes by A. SOMMERFELD. *Demy 8vo, 12s. 6d. net.* RELATIVITY AND THE UNIVERSE. By HARRY SCHMIDT. *Second Edition. Cr. 8vo. 5s. net.*

THE IDEAS OF EINSTEIN'S THEORY. By J. H. THIRRING. *Second Edition. Cr. 8vo. 5s. net.*

THE THEORY OF RELATIVITY. By Prof. ERWIN FREUNDLICH. *Cr. 8vo. 5s. net.*

RELATIVITY FOR ALL. By HERBERT DINGLE. *Third Edition. Fcap. 8vo. 2s. net.*

Evans (Joan). ENGLISH JEWELLERY. *Royal 4to. £2 12s. 6d. net.*

Fitzgerald (Edward). THE RUBA'IYAT OF OMAR KHAYYAM. An edition illustrated by EDMUND J. SULLIVAN. *Wide Cr. 8vo. 10s. 6d. net.*

Fyleman (Rose). FAIRIES AND CHIMNEYS. *Fcap. 8vo. Eighteenth Edition. 3s. 6d. net.*

THE FAIRY GREEN. *Tenth Edition. Fcap. 8vo. 3s. 6d. net.*

THE FAIRY FLUTE. *Sixth Edition. Fcap. 8vo. 3s. 6d. net.*

THE RAINBOW CAT AND OTHER STORIES. *Fcap. 8vo. 3s. 6d. net.*

A SMALL CRUSE. *Fcap. 8vo. 4s. 6d. net.*

FORTY GOOD-NIGHT TALES. *Third Edition. Fcap. 8vo. 3s. 6d. net.*

THE ROSE FYLEMAN FAIRY BOOK. Illustrated. *Cr. 4to. 10s. 6d. net.*

Gibbins (H. de B.). INDUSTRY IN ENGLAND : HISTORICAL OUTLINES. With Maps and Plans. *Tenth Edition. Demy 8vo. 12s. 6d. net.*

THE INDUSTRIAL HISTORY OF ENGLAND. With 5 Maps and a Plan. *Twenty-seventh Edition. Cr. 8vo. 5s.*

Gibbon (Edward). THE DECLINE AND FALL OF THE ROMAN EMPIRE. Edited, with Notes, Appendices, and Maps, by J. B. BURY. *Seven Volumes. Demy 8vo.* Illustrated. *Each 12s. 6d. net. Also in Seven Volumes.* Unillustrated. *Cr. 8vo. Each 7s. 6d. net.*

Glover (T. R.)—
THE CONFLICT OF RELIGIONS IN THE EARLY ROMAN EMPIRE, 10s. 6d. net. POETS AND PURITANS, 10s. 6d. net. FROM PERICLES TO PHILIP, 10s. 6d. net. VIRGIL, 10s. 6d. net. THE CHRISTIAN TRADITION AND ITS VERIFICATION (The Angus Lecture for 1912). 6s. net.

Graham (Harry). MORE DEPORTMENTAL DITTIES. Illustrated by "FISH." *Crown 4to. 10s. 6d. net.*

Grahame (Kenneth). THE WIND IN THE WILLOWS. *Fourteenth Edition. Cr. 8vo. 7s. 6d. net.*
Also Illustrated by NANCY BARNHART. *Small 4to. 10s. 6d. net.*

Hadfield (J. A.). PSYCHOLOGY AND MORALS : An Analysis of Character. *Third Edition. Cr. 8vo. 6s. net.*

Hall (H. R.). THE ANCIENT HISTORY OF THE NEAR EAST FROM THE EARLIEST TIMES TO THE BATTLE OF SALAMIS. Illustrated. *Fifth Edition, Revised. Demy 8vo. 21s. net.*

Hind, (A. M.). A CATALOGUE OF REMBRANDT'S ETCHINGS. *Two vols.* Illustrated. *Wide Royal 8vo. £1, 15s. net.*

Holdsworth (W. S.). A HISTORY OF ENGLISH LAW. *Seven Volumes. Demy 8vo. Each 25s. net.*

Inge (W. R.). CHRISTIAN MYSTICISM (The Bampton Lectures of 1899). *Fifth Edition. Cr. 8vo. 7s. 6d. net.*

Jenks (E.). AN OUTLINE OF ENGLISH LOCAL GOVERNMENT. *Fifth Edition. Cr. 8vo. 5s. net.*

A SHORT HISTORY OF ENGLISH LAW : FROM THE EARLIEST TIMES TO THE END OF THE YEAR 1911. *Second Edition. Demy 8vo. 12s. 6d. net.*

Julian (Lady) of Norwich. REVELATIONS OF DIVINE LOVE. Edited by GRACE WARRACK. *Eighth Edition. Cr. 8vo. 5s. net.*

Keats (John). POEMS. Edited, with Introduction and Notes, by E. DE SELINCOURT. With a Frontispiece in Photogravure. *Fourth Edition. Demy 8vo. 12s. 6d. net.*

Kidd (Benjamin). THE SCIENCE OF POWER. *Ninth Edition. Cr. 8vo. 7s. 6d. net.*

SOCIAL EVOLUTION. *Demy 8vo. 8s. 6d. net.*

Kipling (Rudyard). BARRACK-ROOM BALLADS. 233*rd Thousand. Cr. 8vo. Buckram, 7s. 6d. net. Also Fcap. 8vo. Cloth, 6s. net; leather, 7s. 6d. net.*
Also a Service Edition. *Two Volumes. Square Fcap. 8vo. Each 3s. net.*

THE SEVEN SEAS. 172*nd Thousand. Cr. 8vo. Buckram, 7s. 6d. net. Also Fcap. 8vo. Cloth, 6s. net; leather, 7s. 6d. net.*
Also a Service Edition. *Two Volumes. Square Fcap. 8vo. Each 3s. net.*

THE FIVE NATIONS. 138*th Thousand. Cr. 8vo. Buckram, 7s. 6d. net. Also Fcap. 8vo. Cloth, 6s. net; leather, 7s. 6d. net.*
Also a Service Edition. *Two Volumes. Square Fcap. 8vo. Each 3s. net.*

DEPARTMENTAL DITTIES. '103*rd Thousand. Cr. 8vo. Buckram, 7s. 6d. net. Also Fcap. 8vo. Cloth, 6s. net; leather, 7s. 6d. net.*
Also a Service Edition. *Two Volumes. Square Fcap. 8vo. Each 3s. net.*

THE YEARS BETWEEN. 95*th Thousand. Cr. 8vo. Buckram, 7s. 6d. net. Fcap. 8vo. Cloth, 6s. net; leather, 7s. 6d. net.*
Also a Service Edition. *Two Volumes. Square Fcap. 8vo. Each 3s. net.*

A KIPLING ANTHOLOGY—VERSE. *Third Edition. Fcap. 8vo. Cloth, 6s. net. Leather, 7s. 6d. net.*

TWENTY POEMS FROM RUDYARD KIPLING. 376*th Thousand. Fcap. 8vo. 1s. net.*

Lamb (Charles and Mary). THE COMPLETE WORKS. Edited by E. V. LUCAS. *A New and Revised Edition in Six Volumes. With Frontispieces. Fcap. 8vo. Each 6s. net.*
The volumes are :—
I. MISCELLANEOUS PROSE. II. ELIA AND

THE LAST ESSAYS OF ELIA. III. BOOKS FOR CHILDREN. IV. PLAYS AND POEMS. V. and VI. LETTERS.

Lankester (Sir Ray). SCIENCE FROM AN EASY CHAIR. Illustrated. *Fifteenth Edition. Cr. 8vo. 7s. 6d. net.*
SCIENCE FROM AN EASY CHAIR. *Second Series.* Illustrated. *Third Edition. Cr. 8vo. 7s. 6d. net.*
DIVERSIONS OF A NATURALIST. Illustrated. *Third Edition. Cr. 8vo. 7s. 6d. net.*
SECRETS OF EARTH AND SEA. *Second Edition. Cr. 8vo. 8s. 6d. net.*
GREAT AND SMALL THINGS. Illustrated. *Cr. 8vo. 7s. 6d. net.*

Lescarboura (A. C.). RADIO FOR EVERYBODY. Illustrated. *Cr. 8vo. 7s. 6d. net.*

Lodge (Sir Oliver). MAN AND THE UNIVERSE. *Ninth Edition. Cr. 8vo. 7s. 6d. net.*
THE SURVIVAL OF MAN: A STUDY IN UNRECOGNIZED HUMAN FACULTY. *Seventh Edition. Cr. 8vo. 7s. 6d. net.*
RAYMOND; OR LIFE AND DEATH. Illustrated. *Twelfth Edition. Demy 8vo. 10s. 6d. net.*
RAYMOND REVISED. (Abbreviated edition.) *Cr. 8vo. 6s. net.*

Lorimer (Norma). BY THE WATERS OF EGYPT. Illustrated. *Fourth Edition. Cr. 8vo. 7s. 6d. net.*

Loring (F. H.). ATOMIC THEORIES. *Second Edition. Demy 8vo. 12s. 6d. net.*
THE CHEMICAL ELEMENTS. *Demy 8vo. 8s. 6d. net.*

Lucas (E. V.)—
THE LIFE OF CHARLES LAMB, 2 vols., 21s. net. EDWIN AUSTIN ABBEY, R.A. 2 vols. £6, 6s. net. VERMEER OF DELFT, 10s. 6d. net. A WANDERER IN HOLLAND, 10s 6d. net. A WANDERER IN LONDON, 10s. 6d. net. LONDON REVISITED, 10s. 6d. net. A WANDERER IN PARIS, 10s. 6d. net. A WANDERER IN FLORENCE, 10s. 6d. net. A WANDERER IN VENICE, 10s. 6d. net. THE OPEN ROAD: A Little Book for Wayfarers, 6s. 6d. net. Also an edition illustrated by Claude A. Shepperson, 10s. 6d. net. THE FRIENDLY TOWN: A Little Book for the Urbane, 6s. net. FIRESIDE AND SUNSHINE, 6s. net. CHARACTER AND COMEDY, 6s. net. THE GENTLEST ART: A Choice of Letters by Entertaining Hands, 6s. 6d. net. THE SECOND POST, 6s. net. HER INFINITE VARIETY: A Feminine Portrait Gallery, 6s. net. GOOD COMPANY: A Rally of Men, 6s. net. ONE DAY AND ANOTHER, 6s. net. OLD LAMPS FOR NEW, 6s. net. LOITERER'S HARVEST, 6s. net. CLOUD AND SILVER, 6s. net. A BOSWELL OF BAGHDAD, AND OTHER ESSAYS, 6s. net. 'TWIXT EAGLE AND DOVE, 6s. net. THE PHANTOM JOURNAL, AND OTHER ESSAYS AND DIVERSIONS, 6s. net. GIVING AND RECEIVING, 6s. net. LUCK OF THE YEAR, 6s. net. SPECIALLY SELECTED: A Choice of Essays, 7s. 6d. net. URBANITIES. Illus-

trated by G. L. STAMPA, 7s. 6d. net YOU KNOW WHAT PEOPLE ARE. 5s. net. THE BRITISH SCHOOL: An Anecdotal Guide to the British Painters and Paintings in the National Gallery, 6s. net. ROVING EAST AND ROVING WEST: Notes gathered in India, Japan, and America. 5s. net. See also Dolls' House (The Queen's).

Lynd (Robert). THE BLUE LION and Other Essays. *Fcap 8vo. 6s. net.*
THE PEAL OF BELLS. *Fcap. 8vo. 6s. net.*

Masefield (John). ON THE SPANISH MAIN. *A new edition. Cr. 8vo. 8s. 6d. net.*
A SAILOR'S GARLAND. *A New Edition. Fcap. 8vo. 6s. net.*
SEA LIFE IN NELSON'S TIME. Illustrated. *Second Edition. Cr. 8vo. 5s. net.*

Meldrum (D. S.). REMBRANDT'S PAINTINGS. *Wide Royal 8vo. £3, 3s. net.*

Methuen (A.). AN ANTHOLOGY OF MODERN VERSE. With Introduction by ROBERT LYND. *Fifteenth Edition. Fcap. 8vo. 6s. net. Thin paper, leather, 7s. 6d. net.*
SHAKESPEARE TO HARDY: AN ANTHOLOGY OF ENGLISH LYRICS. With an Introduction by ROBERT LYND. *Third Edition. Fcap. 8vo, 6s. net. Leather, 7s. 6d. net.*

McDougall (William). AN INTRODUCTION TO SOCIAL PSYCHOLOGY. *Eighteenth Edition. Cr. 8vo. 8s. 6d. net.*
NATIONAL WELFARE AND NATIONAL DECAY. *Cr. 8vo. 6s. net.*
AN OUTLINE OF PSYCHOLOGY. *Demy 8vo. 12s. net.*
BODY AND MIND: A HISTORY AND A DEFENCE OF ANIMISM. *Fifth Edition. Demy 8vo. 12s. 6d. net.*
ETHICS AND SOME MODERN WORLD PROBLEMS. *Crown 8vo. 7s. 6d. net.*

Maeterlinck (Maurice)—
THE BLUE BIRD: A Fairy Play in Six Acts. 6s. net. Also an edition illustrated by F. Cayley Robinson, 10s. 6d. net. MARY MAGDALENE: A Play in Three Acts, 5s. net. DEATH, 3s. 6d. net. OUR ETERNITY; 6s. net. THE UNKNOWN GUEST, 6s. net. POEMS, 5s. net. THE WRACK OF THE STORM, 6s. net. THE MIRACLE OF ST. ANTHONY: A Play in One Act, 3s. 6d. net. THE BURGOMASTER OF STILEMONDE: A Play in Three Acts, 5s. net. THE BETROTHAL; or, The Blue Bird Chooses, 6s. net. MOUNTAIN PATHS, 6s. net. THE STORY OF TYLTYL, 21s. net. THE GREAT SECRET. 7s. 6d. net. THE CLOUD THAT LIFTED, and THE POWER OF THE DEAD. 7s. 6d. net.

Milne (A. A.)—
NOT THAT IT MATTERS. *Fcap. 8vo. 6s. net.* IF I MAY. *Fcap. 8vo. 6s. net.*

Newman (Tom). HOW TO PLAY BILLIARDS. Illustrated. *Cr. 8vo, 8s. 6d. net.*

Oxenham (John)—
BEES IN AMBER; A Little Book of Thoughtful Verse. *Small Pott 8vo.*

Stiff Boards. 2s. *net.* ALL'S WELL ; A Collection of War Poems. THE KING'S HIGH WAY. THE VISION SPLENDID. THE FIERY CROSS. HIGH ALTARS : The Record of a Visit to the Battlefields of France and Flanders. HEARTS COURAGEOUS. ALL CLEAR ! *All Small Pott 8vo. Paper,* 1s. 3d. *net ; cloth boards,* 2s. *net.* WINDS OF THE DAWN. 2s. *net.*

Perry (W. J.). THE CHILDREN OF THE SUN : A STUDY IN THE EARLY HISTORY OF CIVILIZATION. *Demy 8vo.* 18s. *net.*

THE ORIGIN OF MAGIC AND RELIGION. *Crown 8vo.* 6s. *net.*

THE GROWTH OF CIVILIZATION. *Crown 8vo.* 6s. *net.*

Petrie (W. M. Flinders). A HISTORY OF EGYPT. Illustrated. *Six Volumes. Cr. 8vo. Each* 9s. *net.*

VOL. I. FROM THE 1ST TO THE XVITH DYNASTY. *Tenth Edition.* (12s. *net.*)

VOL. II. THE XVIITH AND XVIIITH DYNASTIES. *Sixth Edition.*

VOL. III. XIXTH TO XXXTH DYNASTIES. *Second Edition.*

VOL. IV. EGYPT UNDER THE PTOLEMAIC DYNASTY. J. P. MAHAFFY. *Second Edition.*

VOL. V. EGYPT UNDER ROMAN RULE. J. G. MILNE. *Second Edition.*

VOL. VI. EGYPT IN THE MIDDLE AGES. STANLEY LANE POOLE. *Second Edition.*

SYRIA AND EGYPT, FROM THE TELL EL AMARNA LETTERS. *Cr. 8vo.* 5s. *net.*

EGYPTIAN TALES. Translated from the Papyri. First Series, 1VTH to XIITH Dynasty. Illustrated. *Third Edition. Cr. 8vo.* 5s. *net.*

EGYPTIAN TALES. Translated from the Papyri. Second Series, XVIIITH to XIXTH Dynasty. Illustrated. *Second Edition. Cr. 8vo.* 5s. *net.*

Pollitt (Arthur W.). THE ENJOYMENT OF MUSIC. *Second Edition. Cr. 8vo.* 5s. *net.*

Ponsonby (Arthur). ENGLISH DIARIES. *Second Edition. Demy 8vo.* 21s. *net.*

Price (L. L.). A SHORT HISTORY OF POLITICAL ECONOMY IN ENGLAND FROM ADAM SMITH TO ARNOLD TOYNBEE. *Eleventh Edition. Cr. 8vo.* 5s. *net.*

Robinson (W. Heath). HUMOURS OF GOLF. *Demy 4to.* 7s. 6d. *net.*

Selous (Edmund)—
TOMMY SMITH'S ANIMALS. TOMMY SMITH'S OTHER ANIMALS. TOMMY SMITH AT THE ZOO. TOMMY SMITH AGAIN AT THE ZOO. *Each* 2s. 9d. TOMMY SMITH'S BIRDS, 2s. 6d. JACK'S INSECTS, 3s. 6d. JACK'S OTHER INSECTS, 3s. 6d.

Smith (Adam). THE WEALTH OF NATIONS. Edited by EDWIN CANNAN. *Two Volumes. Third Edition. Demy 8vo.* £1 5s. *net.*

Smith (C. Fox).
SAILOR TOWN DAYS. SEA SONGS AND BALLADS. A BOOK OF FAMOUS SHIPS. All Illustrated. *Cr. 8vo.* 6s. *net. each.*

Sommerfeld (Arnold). ATOMIC STRUCTURE AND SPECTRAL LINES. *Demy 8vo.* 32s. *net.*

Stevenson (R. L.). THE LETTERS OF ROBERT LOUIS STEVENSON. Edited by Sir SIDNEY COLVIN. *A New Rearranged Edition in four volumes. Fourth Edition. Fcap. 8vo. Each* 6s. *net.*

Surtees (R. S.)—
HANDLEY CROSS, 7s. 6d. *net.* MR. SPONGE'S SPORTING TOUR, 7s. 6d. *net.* ASK MAMMA : or, The Richest Commoner in England, 7s. 6d. *net.* JORROCKS'S JAUNTS AND JOLLITIES, 6s. *net.* MR. FACEY ROMFORD'S HOUNDS, 7s. 6d. *net.* HAWBUCK GRANGE ; or, The Sporting Adventures of Thomas Scott, Esq., 6s. *net.* PLAIN OR RINGLETS ? 7s. 6d. *net.* HILLINGDON HALL, 7s. 6d. *net.*

Tatchell (Frank). THE HAPPY TRAVELLER : A BOOK FOR POOR MEN. *Third Edition. Cr. 8vo.* 7s. 6d. *net.*

Thomson (J. Arthur). WHAT IS MAN ? *Second Edition. Cr. 8vo.* 6s. 6d. *net.*

Tilden (W. T.). THE ART OF LAWN TENNIS. Illustrated. *Fifth Edition. Cr. 8vo.* 6s. *net.*

Tileston (Mary W.). DAILY STRENGTH FOR DAILY NEEDS. *Twenty-ninth Edition. Medium 16mo.* 3s. 6d. *net.*

Underhill (Evelyn). MYSTICISM. A Study in the Nature and Development of Man's Spiritual Consciousness. *Tenth Edition. Demy 8vo.* 15s. *net.*

THE LIFE OF THE SPIRIT AND THE LIFE OF TO-DAY. *Fifth Edition. Cr. 8vo.* 7s. 6d. *net.*

Vardon (Harry). HOW TO PLAY GOLF. Illustrated. *Eighteenth Edition. Cr. 8vo.* 5s. *net.*

Wade (G. W.). NEW TESTAMENT HISTORY. *Demy 8vo.* 18s. *net.*

OLD TESTAMENT HISTORY. *Ninth Edition. Cr. 8vo.* 7s. 6d. *net.*

Wayne (Philip). A CHILD'S BOOK OF LYRICS. *Second Edition. Fcap. 8vo.* 3s. 6d. *net.*

Waterhouse (Elizabeth). A LITTLE BOOK OF LIFE AND DEATH. *Twenty-second Edition. Small Pott 8vo.* 2s. 6d. *net.*

Wegener (A.). THE ORIGIN OF CONTINENTS AND OCEANS. *Demy 8vo.* 10s. 6d. *net.*

Wells (J.). A SHORT HISTORY OF ROME. *Eighteenth Edition.* With 3 Maps. *Cr. 8vo.* 5s.

Wilde (Oscar). THE WORKS OF OSCAR WILDE. *Fcap. 8vo. Each* 6s. 6d. *net.*
I. LORD ARTHUR SAVILE'S CRIME AND THE PORTRAIT OF MR. W. H. II. THE DUCHESS OF PADUA. III. POEMS. IV. LADY WINDERMERE'S FAN. V. A WOMAN OF NO IMPORTANCE. VI. AN IDEAL HUSBAND. VII. THE IMPORTANCE OF BEING EARNEST. VIII. A HOUSE OF POMEGRANATES. IX. INTENTIONS. X. DE PRO-

FUNDIS AND PRISON LETTERS. XI. ESSAYS. XII. SALOME, A FLORENTINE TRAGEDY, and LA SAINTE COURTISANE. XIII. A CRITIC IN PALL MALL. XIV. SELECTED PROSE OF OSCAR WILDE.

XV. ART AND DECORATION. XVI. FOR LOVE OF THE KING : A Burmese Masque (5s. net.).

Yeats (W. B.). A BOOK OF IRISH VERSE. *Fourth Edition. Cr. 8vo. 7s. net.*

PART II.—A SELECTION OF SERIES

The Antiquary's Books

Demy 8vo. 10s. 6d. net each volume. With Numerous Illustrations

ANCIENT PAINTED GLASS IN ENGLAND. ARCHÆOLOGY AND FALSE ANTIQUITIES. THE BELLS OF ENGLAND. THE BRASSES OF ENGLAND. THE CASTLES AND WALLED TOWNS OF ENGLAND. CELTIC ART IN PAGAN AND CHRISTIAN TIMES. CHURCHWARDENS' ACCOUNTS. THE DOMESDAY INQUEST. ENGLISH CHURCH FURNITURE. ENGLISH COSTUME. ENGLISH MONASTIC LIFE. ENGLISH SEALS. FOLK-LORE AS AN HISTORICAL SCIENCE. THE GUILDS AND COMPANIES OF LONDON. THE HERMITS AND ANCHORITES OF ENGLAND. THE MANOR AND MANORIAL RECORDS. THE MEDIÆVAL HOSPITALS OF ENGLAND. OLD ENGLISH INSTRUMENTS OF MUSIC. OLD ENGLISH LIBRARIES. OLD SERVICE BOOKS OF THE ENGLISH CHURCH. PARISH LIFE IN MEDIÆVAL ENGLAND. THE PARISH REGISTERS OF ENGLAND. REMAINS OF THE PREHISTORIC AGE IN ENGLAND. THE ROMAN ERA IN BRITAIN. ROMANO-BRITISH BUILDINGS AND EARTHWORKS. THE ROYAL FORESTS OF ENGLAND. THE SCHOOLS OF MEDIÆVAL ENGLAND. SHRINES OF BRITISH SAINTS.

The Arden Shakespeare

General Editor, R. H. CASE

Demy 8vo. 6s. net each volume

An edition of Shakespeare in Single Plays ; each edited with a full Introduction, Textual Notes, and a Commentary at the foot of the page.

The Arden Shakespeare has now been completed by the publication of MUCH ADO ABOUT NOTHING. Edited by GRACE R. TRENERY.

Classics of Art

Edited by DR. J. H. W. LAING

With numerous Illustrations. Wide Royal 8vo

THE ART OF THE GREEKS, 21s. net. THE ART OF THE ROMANS, 16s. net. CHARDIN, 15s. net. DONATELLO, 16s. net. FLORENTINE SCULPTORS, 21s. net. GEORGE ROMNEY, 15s. net. GHIRLANDAIO, 15s. net. LAWRENCE, 25s. net. MICHELANGELO, 21s. net. RAPHAEL, 15s. net. REMBRANDT'S PAINTINGS, 63s. net. RUBENS, 30s. net. TINTORETTO, 16s. net. TITIAN, 16s. net. TURNER'S SKETCHES AND DRAWINGS, 15s. net. VELASQUEZ, 15s. net.

The " Complete " Series

Fully Illustrated. Demy 8vo

THE COMPLETE AIRMAN, 16s. net. THE COMPLETE ATHLETIC TRAINER, 10s. 6d. net. THE COMPLETE BILLIARD PLAYER, 10s. 6d. net. THE COMPLETE COOK, 10s. 6d. net. THE COMPLETE FOXHUNTER, 16s. net. THE COMPLETE GOLFER, 12s. 6d. net. THE COMPLETE HOCKEY PLAYER, 10s. 6d. net. THE COMPLETE HORSEMAN, 15s. net. THE COMPLETE JUJITSUAN. (Cr. 8vo.) 5s. net. THE COMPLETE LAWN TENNIS PLAYER, 12s. 6d. net. THE COMPLETE MOTORIST, 10s. 6d. net. THE COMPLETE MOUNTAINEER, 18s. net. THE COMPLETE OARSMAN, 15s. net. THE COMPLETE PHOTOGRAPHER, 12s. 6d. net. THE COMPLETE RUGBY FOOTBALLER, ON THE NEW ZEALAND SYSTEM, 12s. 6d. net. THE COMPLETE SHOT, 16s. net. THE COMPLETE SWIMMER, 10s. 6d. net. THE COMPLETE YACHTSMAN, 15s. net.

The Connoisseur's Library

With numerous Illustrations. Wide Royal 8vo. £1, 11s. 6d. net each volume

ENGLISH COLOURED BOOKS. ETCHINGS. EUROPEAN ENAMELS. FINE BOOKS. GLASS. GOLDSMITHS' AND SILVERSMITHS' WORK. ILLUMINATED MANUSCRIPTS.

IVORIES. JEWELLERY. MEZZOTINTS. MINIATURES. PORCELAIN. SEALS. WOOD SCULPTURE.

Health Series

Fcap. 8vo. 2s. 6d. net

THE BABY. THE CARE OF THE BODY. THE CARE OF THE TEETH. THE EYES OF OUR CHILDREN. HEALTH FOR THE MIDDLE-AGED. THE HEALTH OF A WOMAN. THE HEALTH OF THE SKIN. HOW TO LIVE

LONG. THE PREVENTION OF THE COMMON COLD. STAYING THE PLAGUE. THROAT AND EAR TROUBLES. TUBERCULOSIS. THE HEALTH OF THE CHILD, 2s. net.

The Library of Devotion

Handy Editions of the great Devotional Books, well edited

With Introductions and (where necessary) Notes

Small Pott 8vo, cloth, 3s. net and 3s. 6d. net

Little Books on Art

With many Illustrations. Demy 16mo. 5s. net each volume

Each volume consists of about 200 pages, and contains from 30 to 40

Illustrations, including a Frontispiece in Photogravure

ALBRECHT DÜRER. THE ARTS OF JAPAN. BOOKPLATES. BOTTICELLI. BURNE-JONES. CELLINI. CHRIST IN ART. CLAUDE. CONSTABLE. COROT. EARLY ENGLISH WATER-COLOUR. ENAMELS. FREDERIC LEIGHTON. GEORGE ROMNEY. GREEK ART. GREUZE

AND BOUCHER. HOLBEIN. ILLUMINATED MANUSCRIPTS. JEWELLERY. JOHN HOPPNER. Sir JOSHUA REYNOLDS. MILLET. MINIATURES. OUR LADY IN ART. RAPHAEL. RODIN. TURNER. VANDYCK. WATTS.

The Little Guides

With many Illustrations by E. H. NEW and other artists, and from photographs

Small Pott 8vo. 4s. net to 7s. 6d. net

Guides to the English and Welsh Counties, and some well-known districts.

The main features of these Guides are (1) a handy and charming form; (2) illustrations from photographs and by well-known artists; (3) good plans and maps; (4) an adequate but compact presentation of everything that is interesting in the natural features, history, archæology, and architecture of the town or district treated.

Plays

Fcap. 8vo. 3s. 6d. net

MILESTONES. Arnold Bennett and Edward Knoblock. *Eleventh Edition.*
IDEAL HUSBAND, AN. Oscar Wilde. *Acting Edition.*
KISMET. Edward Knoblock. *Fourth Edition.*
WARE CASE, THE. George Pleydell.

THE GREAT ADVENTURE. Arnold Bennett. *Fifth Edition.*
GENERAL POST. J. E. Harold Terry. *Second Edition.*
THE HONEYMOON. Arnold Bennett. *Third Edition.*

Sport Series
Illustrated.   Fcap. 8vo

All About Flying, 3s. net. Alpine Ski-ing at All Heights and Seasons, 5s. net. Ski-ing for Beginners, 5s. net. Golf Do's and Dont's, 2s. net. Quick Cuts to Good Golf, 2s. net. Inspired Golf, 2s. 6d. net. Driving, Approaching, Putting, 2s. net. Golf Clubs and How to Use Them, 2s. net. The Secret of Golf for Occasional Players, 2s. net. The Golfing Swing, 2s. 6d. net. Golf Rules and Decisions. 3s. 6d. net. Lawn Tennis, 2s. 6d. net. Lawn Tennis Do's and Dont's, 2s. 6d. net. Lawn Tennis for Young Players, 2s. 6d. net. Lawn Tennis for Club Players, 2s. 6d. net. Lawn Tennis for Match Players, 2s. 6d. net. Hockey, 4s. net. How to Swim, 2s. net. Punting, 3s. 6d. net. Skating, 3s. net. Wrestling, 2s. net. The Technique of Lawn Tennis, 2s. 6d. net. The Lawn Tennis Umpire, 2s. 6d. net. Motor Do's and Dont's, 2s. 6d. net. Mah Jong Do's and Dont's, 2s. net. Auction Bridge Do's and Dont's. 3s. net.

Methuen's Half-Crown Library
Crown 8vo.
Cheap Editions of Popular Books
Write for a Complete List

Methuen's Two-Shilling Library
Fcap. 8vo.
Write for a Complete List

Part III.—A Selection of Works of Fiction

Bennett (Arnold)—
Clayhanger, 8s. net. Hilda Lessways. 8s. 6d. net. These Twain. The Card. The Regent: A Five Towns Story of Adventure in London. The Price of Love. Buried Alive. A Man from the North. Whom God hath Joined. A Great Man: A Frolic. Mr. Prohack. All 7s. 6d. net. The Matador of the Five Towns, 6s. net.

Birmingham (George A.)—
Spanish Gold. The Search Party. The Bad Times. Up, the Rebels. The Lost Lawyer. The Great-Grandmother. Found Money. All 7s. 6d. net. Inisheeny, 8s. 6d. net.

Brandon (John G.)—The Big Heart. Cr. 8vo. 3s. 6d. net.

Burroughs (Edgar Rice)—
Tarzan of the Apes, 6s. net. The Return of Tarzan, 6s. net. The Beasts of Tarzan, 6s. net. The Son of Tarzan, 6s. net. Jungle Tales of Tarzan, 6s. net. Tarzan and the Jewels of Opar, 6s. net. Tarzan the Untamed, 7s. 6d. net. Tarzan and the Golden Lion, 3s. 6d. net. A Princess of Mars, 6s. net. The Gods of Mars, 6s. net. The Warlord of Mars, 6s. net. Thuvia, Maid of Mars, 6s. net. Tarzan the Terrible, 2s. 6d. net. The Mucker, 6s. net. The Man without a Soul, 6s. net. The Chessmen of Mars, 6s. net. At the Earth's Core, 6s. net. Pellucidar, 7s. 6d. net. The Girl from Hollywood, 7s. 6d. net.

Conrad (Joseph)—
A Set of Six, 7s. 6d. net. Victory: An Island Tale. The Secret Agent: A Simple Tale. Under Western Eyes. Chance. All 9s. net.

Corelli (Marie)—
A Romance of Two Worlds, 7s. 6d. net. Vendetta: or, The Story of One Forgotten, 7s. 6d. net. Thelma: A Norwegian Princess, 7s. 6d. net. Ardath: The Story of a Dead Self, 7s. 6d. net. The Soul of Lilith, 7s. 6d. net. Wormwood: A Drama of Paris, 7s. 6d. net. Barabbas: A Dream of the World's Tragedy, 7s. 6d. net. The Sorrows of Satan, 7s. 6d. net. The Master-Christian, 7s. 6d. net. Temporal Power: A Study in Supremacy, 6s. net. God's Good Man: A Simple Love Story, 7s. 6d. net. Holy Orders: The Tragedy of a Quiet Life, 8s. 6d. net. The Mighty Atom, 7s. 6d. net. Boy: A Sketch, 7s. 6d. net. Cameos, 6s. net. The Life Everlasting. 8s. 6d. net. The Love of Long Ago, and Other Stories, 7s. 6d. net. Innocent, 7s. 6d. net. The Secret Power: A Romance of the Time, 6s. net. Love—And the Philosopher: A Study in Sentiment, 6s. net.

Hichens (Robert)—
FELIX : Three Years in a Life, 7s. 6d. net.
THE WOMAN WITH THE FAN, 7s. 6d. net.
THE GARDEN OF ALLAH, 8s. 6d. net. THE
CALL OF THE BLOOD, 8s. 6d. net. THE
DWELLER ON THE THRESHOLD, 7s. 6d.
net. THE WAY OF AMBITION, 7s. 6d. net.
IN THE WILDERNESS, 7s. 6d. net. AFTER
THE VERDICT, 7s. 6d. net.

Hope (Anthony)—
A CHANGE OF AIR. A MAN OF MARK.
SIMON DALE. THE KING'S MIRROR.
THE DOLLY DIALOGUES. MRS. MAXON
PROTESTS. A YOUNG MAN'S YEAR.
BEAUMAROY HOME FROM THE WARS.
All 7s. 6d. net.

Jacobs (W. W.)—
MANY CARGOES, 5s. net. SEA URCHINS, 5s.
net and 3s. 6d. net. A MASTER OF CRAFT,
6s. net. LIGHT FREIGHTS, 6s. net. THE
SKIPPER'S WOOING, 5s. net. AT SUN-
WICH PORT, 5s. net. DIALSTONE LANE,
5s. net. ODD CRAFT, 5s. net. THE LADY
OF THE BARGE, 5s. net. SALTHAVEN, 6s.
net. SAILORS' KNOTS, 5s. net. SHORT
CRUISES, 6s. net.

Knox (R. A.)—
MEMORIES OF THE FUTURE. 7s. 6d. net.
SANCTIONS : A FRIVOLITY. 7s. 6d. net.

London (Jack)—WHITE FANG. Nineteenth
Edition. Cr. 8vo. 7s. 6d. net.

Lucas (E. V.)—
LISTENER'S LURE : An Oblique Narration,
6s. net. OVER BEMERTON'S : An Easy-
going Chronicle, 6s. net. MR. INGLESIDE,
6s. net. LONDON LAVENDER, 6s. net.
LANDMARKS, 6s. net. THE VERMILION
BOX, 6s. net. VERENA IN THE MIDST,
8s. 6d. net. ROSE AND ROSE, 6s. net.
GENEVRA'S MONEY, 7s. 6d. net. ADVISORY
BEN, 7s. 6d. net.

McKenna (Stephen)—
SONIA : Between Two Worlds, 8s. net.
NINETY-SIX HOURS' LEAVE, 7s. 6d. net.
THE SIXTH SENSE, 6s. net. MIDAS & SON,
8s. net.

Malet (Lucas)—
THE HISTORY OF SIR RICHARD CALMADY :
A Romance. 10s. net. THE CARISSIMA.

THE GATELESS BARRIER. DEADHAM
HARD. All 7s. 6d. net. THE WAGES OF
SIN. 8s. net. COLONEL ENDERBY'S WIFE,
7s. 6d. net.

Mason (A. E. W.). CLEMENTINA.
Illustrated. Ninth Edition. 7s. 6d. net.

Milne (A. A.)—
THE DAY'S PLAY. THE HOLIDAY ROUND.
ONCE A WEEK. All 7s. 6d. net. THE
SUNNY SIDE. 6s. net. THE RED HOUSE
MYSTERY. 6s. net.

Oxenham (John)—
THE QUEST OF THE GOLDEN ROSE. MARY
ALL-ALONE. 7s. 6d. net.

Parker (Gilbert)—
THE TRANSLATION OF A SAVAGE. WHEN
VALMOND CAME TO PONTIAC : The Story of
a Lost Napoleon. AN ADVENTURER OF THE
NORTH : The Last Adventures of " Pretty
Pierre." THE SEATS OF THE MIGHTY. THE
BATTLE OF THE STRONG : A Romance of Two
Kingdoms. THE TRAIL OF THE SWORD.
NORTHERN LIGHTS. All 7s. 6d. net.

Phillpotts (Eden)—
CHILDREN OF THE MIST. THE RIVER.
THE HUMAN BOY AND THE WAR. All
7s. 6d. net.

Rohmer (Sax)—
THE GOLDEN SCORPION. 7s. 6d. net. THE
DEVIL DOCTOR. THE MYSTERY OF DR.
FU-MANCHU. THE YELLOW CLAW. All
3s. 6d. net.

Swinnerton (F.). SHOPS AND HOUSES.
SEPTEMBER. THE HAPPY FAMILY. ON
THE STAIRCASE. COQUETTE. THE CHASTE
WIFE. THE THREE LOVERS. All 7s. 6d.
net. THE MERRY HEART. THE CASEMENT.
THE YOUNG IDEA. All 6s. net.

Wells (H. G.). BEALBY. Fourth Edition.
Cr. 8vo. 7s. 6d. net.

Williamson (C. N. and A. M.)—
THE LIGHTNING CONDUCTOR : The Strange
Adventures of a Motor-Car. LADY BETTY
ACROSS THE WATER. IT HAPPENED IN
EGYPT. THE SHOP GIRL. MY FRIEND
THE CHAUFFEUR. SET IN SILVER. THE
GREAT PEARL SECRET. All 7s. 6d. net.
CRUCIFIX CORNER. 6s. net.

Methuen's Half-Crown Novels

Crown 8vo.

Cheap Editions of many of the most Popular Novels of the day
Write for a Complete List

Methuen's Two-Shilling Novels

Fcap. 8vo.

Write for Complete List